FROM THE
COOKBOOKS OF

Book #1 of the Retro Cookbooks Series

Mock Toad-in-the-Hole

and
Other Vintage 'Mock' Dishes

Farrah Knight

Edited by C. Egan

LEAVES OF GOLD PRESS

LEAVES of GOLD PRESS

First published 2012 by Leaves of Gold Press
ABN 67 099 575 078
PO Box 345, Shoreham, 3916
Victoria, Australia

National Library of Australia Cataloguing-in-Publication entry
Author: Knight, Farrah.
Title: Mock toad-in-the-hole : and other vintage 'mock' dishes
by Farrah Knight ; edited by C. Egan.
Cover design by Trish Hart
ISBN: 9780987500113 (paperback.)
ISBN: 9780987369192 (ebook)
Series: Retro cookbooks series ; 1
Notes: Includes bibliographical references and index.
Subjects: Cooking.
Ingredient substitutions (Cooking)
Other Authors/Contributors: Egan, C.
Dewey Number: 641.5

CONTENTS

THE MOCK MENU

Quite a Novelty

"Come to a Mock Meal," ran the dinner invitation.

I accepted, wondering a little whether it would be a sort of mirage entertainment! But not a bit of it. The dinner was a good solid reality (says a correspondent in an exchange).

It began, as I might have expected, with mock turtle soup. This was made from half a calf's head, boiled with the bones (tied in a bag) and the usual soup vegetables for three hours. Strained and clarified, fortified with a little sherry and lemon juice, it might have defied the oldest of aldermen to spot its falsity.

Next came mock goose, a baked dish, made from pigs' fry, onions, sage, and sliced potato. A layer of thin slices of the fry had been put into the dish, next came a layer of potato slices, next a plentiful sprinkling of chopped sage and onion, another layer of the fry, and so on till the dish was full. Followed a cup of water, a dredging of flour, pepper, salt—and cooking in a slow oven. The seasoning had so permeated the dish, and the fry was so tender, that I might have sworn it was goose I was eating.

As an alternative, mock chicken curry was served. The "chicken" was a rabbit, gently stewed and boned before being curried and surrounded with a ring of rice. As tender was 't s any chicken! Our hostess told us that her mock chicken pie was equally successful, and well we believed her.

Mock plum pudding formed the sweet. It was a boiled pudding, made from breadcrumbs mixed with some mince-meat that had been kept over from last December. Our hostess confided the fact that this admirable confection had cost her exactly one shilling, generous though its proportions were.

SUNDAY TIMES (PERTH, WESTERN AUSTRALIA : 1902 - 1954)

SUNDAY 16 AUGUST 1931

The Mock Menu - Quite a Novelty

'"Come to a Mock Meal," ran the dinner invitation. I accepted, wondering a little whether it would be a sort of mirage entertainment! But not a bit of it. The dinner was a good solid reality (says a correspondent in an exchange.

'It began, as I might have expected, with mock turtle soup. This was made from half a calf's head, boiled with the bones (tied in a bag) and the usual soup vegetables for three hours Strained and clarified, fortified with a little sherry and lemon juice, it might have defied the oldest of aldermen to spot its falsity.

'Next came mock goose, a baked dish, made from pigs' fry, onions, sage, and sliced potato... The seasoning had so permeated the dish, and the fry was so tender, that I might have sworn it was goose I was eating.

'As an alternative, mock chicken curry was served. The "chicken" was a rabbit, gently stewed and boned before being curried and surrounded with a ring of rice. As tender was it as any chicken! Our hostess told us that her mock chicken pie was equally successful, and well we believed her.

'Mock plum pudding formed the sweet. It was a boiled pudding, made from breadcrumbs mixed with some mince-meat that had been kept over from last December. Our hostess confided the fact that this admirable confection had cost her exactly one shilling, generous though its proportions were.'

NOTE

Note that this book, being a collection of authentic vintage recipes, should perhaps be treated more as a collection of humorous curiosities than an everyday cookbook. Readers may enjoy simply reading it and revelling in the quaint names (and genuine vintage illustrations from newspapers and magazines), even more than using it as a cookery instruction manual!

FOREWORD

Mock Turtle Soup was famously mentioned in Lewis Carroll's classic tale 'Alice in Wonderland', but due to the fact that Carroll invented a creature called a Mock Turtle, many people today believe the dish is purely fictitious!

Certainly there is no such creature, but the real soup recipe can be found in Mrs. Beeton's renowned 19th century cookery book, and now within the pages of this recent collection—along with better-known taste-tempters such as mock cream and mock chicken.

Poverty and frugality were the mothers of many 'mock' dishes, as were crop failures and war. During wartime, governments introduced rationing to cope with food shortages. For example in Great Britain during the Second World War meat, cheese, butter, margarine, bacon and ham, eggs, tea, preserves, sugar and cooking fats such as lard were scarce and rationed. One fresh egg per week per person was allowed, or one packet of dried eggs per person every four weeks. As a result, many wartime dishes were made without eggs.

To aid home cooks, the British Ministry of Food published 'austerity recipes' in newspapers, using ingredients that were readily available. People experimented, using cheap ingredients to produce expensive flavours. Newspapers ran recipe competitions, in which many inventive cooks took part.

Most of the old recipes have been reproduced here exactly as they originally appeared, so if you wish to change the measurements, consult the handy guide in the back of this book.

Now you, too, can save money and astonish your dinner guests with

MOCK TOAD-IN-THE-HOLE
AND OTHER VINTAGE MOCK DISHES

PS If anyone can help find the following lost wartime recipes, please contact the publisher!

Mock Creamed Rice, Mock Tea, Mock Sweetcorn, Mock Sago and Mock Caviar.

1
MOCK TURTLE SOUPS

Mock Turtle Soup 1861

A knuckle of veal weighing 5 or 6 lbs.,
2 cow-heels,
2 large onions stuck with cloves,
1 bunch of sweet herbs,
3 blades of mace,
salt to taste,
12 peppercorns,
1 glass of sherry,
24 force-meat balls,
A little lemon-juice,
4 quarts of water.

Put all the ingredients, except the force-meat balls and lemon-juice, in an earthen jar, and stew for 6 hours. Do not open it till cold. When wanted for use, skim off all the fat, and strain carefully; place it on the fire, cut up the meat into inch-and-a-half squares, put it, with the force-meat balls and lemon juice, into the soup, and serve. It can be flavoured with a tablespoonful of anchovy, or Harvey's sauce.

Notes
Time -- 6 hours.
Average cost - 1 shilling and 4 pence per quart.
Seasonable in winter.
Sufficient for 10 persons.

SOURCE: MRS BEETON, 1861.

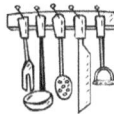

Mock Turtle Soup 1884

Take a calf's head, cut it in half, clean it well and then boil it until half done; cut all the meat off in small square pieces, break the bones of the head and put back in the kettle.

Fry some shallots in butter, and dredge in flour; when it is nicely browned put it into the kettle and let it boil gently for one hour; skim well.

About ten minutes before serving, season with basil, tarragon, parsley, cayenne pepper, and salt to your taste; also two tablespoon-fuls of mushroom catsup (ketchup) and one pint of Madeira wine.

This will make four quarts of splendid soup.

SOURCE: MRS FRANCES WILLEY, 1884

Mock Turtle Soup 1905

Stew a shank of veal weighing 5 lb to 6 lb in a large earthen jar, with two cow heels, two onions stuck with one clove each, one bunch of herbs, three blades of mace, a few peppercorns. a little salt, and a glass of sherry, for about six hours, in four quarts of water.

Allow this to cool in the jar, and when quite cold remove the fat from the top, strain the soup, cut the meat into small squares, and put all back, except the onions and herbs, into a stew pan, with about eighteen small forcemeat balls and the juice of a lemon.

If liked, a little mushroom ketchup may be added.

Note: For forcemeat balls, see 'Mock Forcemeat' recipe.

SOURCE: MORNING BULLETIN 1905

Mock Turtle Soup 1918

1 calf's head
2 cups brown stock
6 cloves
¼ cup butter
½ teaspoon peppercorns
½ cup flour
6 allspice berries
1 cup stewed and strained tomatoes
2 sprigs thyme
1/3 cup sliced onion
Juice ½ lemon
1/3 cup carrot, cut in dice
Madeira wine
Royal Custard (see below)
Egg Balls (see below)

Clean and wash calf's head; soak one hour in cold water to cover. Cook until tender in three quarts boiling salted water (to which seasoning and vegetables have been added). Remove head; boil stock until reduced to one quart. Strain and cool. Melt and brown butter, add flour, and stir until well browned; then pour on slowly brown stock. Add head-stock, tomato, one cup face-meat cut in dice, and lemon juice. Simmer five minutes; add Royal Custard cut in dice, and Egg Balls, or Force-meat Balls. Add Madeira wine, and salt and pepper to taste.

Royal Custard
Yolks 3 eggs
1/8 teaspoon salt
1 egg
Slight grating nutmeg
½ cup Consommé
Few grains cayenne

Beat eggs slightly, add Consommé and seasonings. Pour into a small buttered tin mould, place in pan of hot water, and bake until firm; cool, remove from mould, and cut in fancy shapes.

Egg Balls I
Yolks 2 "hard-boiled" eggs
Few grains cayenne
1/8 teaspoon salt
½ teaspoon melted butter

Rub yolks through sieve, add seasonings, and moisten with raw egg yolk to make of consistency to handle. Shape in small balls, roll in flour, and sauté in butter. Serve in Brown Soup Stock, Consommé, or Mock Turtle Soup.

Egg Balls II
1 "hard-boiled" egg
Few grains cayenne
1/8 teaspoon salt
1 teaspoon heavy cream
¼ teaspoon finely chopped parsley

Rub yolk through a sieve, add white finely chopped, and remaining ingredients. Add raw egg yolk to make mixture of right consistency to handle. Shape in small balls, and poach in boiling water or stock.

SOURCE: MRS FARMER, 1918.

Mock Turtle Soup 1921

1 calf's head
4 lbs knuckle of veal
1 lb marrow bone
4 quarts cold water
1 small sliced carrot
2 sliced onions
3 sprigs thyme
2 sprigs marjoram
Bit of bay leaf
½ teaspoon clove
½ teaspoon peppercorns
1/8 teaspoon celery seed
4 allspice berries
2 blades mace
½ tablespoon salt
1 ½ tablespoons butter
1 ½ tablespoons flour
1 ½ tablespoons lemon juice
¼ cup Sherry wine
Salt and pepper

Clean and wash calf's head, put in kettle with veal and marrow bone; add cold water, cover, bring slowly to boiling point and let simmer until meat leaves bone. Cut face meat in one-half inch cubes -- there should be one cup -- and set aside with brains to use as garnish. Put tongue, remaining calf's head meat and veal through meat chopper. Return to kettle containing stock and add vegetables and seasonings and let simmer two hours. Strain, cool, remove fat, reheat and add butter and flour browned together. Add meat, lemon juice, sherry and salt and pepper to taste. Then add egg balls.

Egg Balls III

Mash yolks of three hard-boiled eggs and add an equal measure of mashed calf's brains. Season highly with salt and pepper and add enough slightly beaten egg to hold mixture so that it may be shaped into small balls. Roll balls in flour and sauté in butter.

SOURCE: FARMER 1921

Mock Turtle Soup 1929

Half a Calf's Head

2 lb Shin of Beef

1 Onion

1 small Carrot

24 Peppercorns

6 Cloves

1 Bay Leaf

1 blade Mace

1 sprig Parsley

1 sprig Marjoram, and a little Basil.

Cut up beef, and clean head thoroughly. Take out brains and tongue, and put in salt and water. Put head, beef, and bones in a pan with 3 quarts water and 1 tablespoonful salt, and boil 6 hours. Remove fat; add tiny bit of all the vegetables to refresh the flavour. Thicken by mixing 2 oz. cornflour, 1 teacupful of water and a little ketchup, and stir till boiling; add some pieces of the head, cut into little square pieces, and the juice of 1 lemon, and serve with a dust of cayenne pepper and squares of toast.

SOURCE: KIRK, 1929

2
OTHER MOCK SOUPS

Mock Bisque Soup

2 cups raw or canned tomatoes
Bit of bay leaf
2 teaspoons sugar
¾ cup stale bread crumbs
1/3 teaspoon soda
4 cups milk
½ onion, stuck with 6 cloves
½ tablespoon salt
Sprig of parsley
1/8 teaspoon pepper
1/3 cup butter

Scald milk with bread crumbs, onion, parsley, and bay leaf. Remove seasonings and rub through a sieve.
Cook tomatoes with sugar fifteen minutes; add soda and rub through a sieve. Reheat bread and milk to boiling-point, add tomatoes, and pour at once into tureen over butter, salt, and pepper. Serve with croûtons, crisp crackers, or souffléd crackers.

SOURCE: MRS FARMER, 1918

Mock Bouillon

2 quart-cans tomatoes
3 cloves
2 cups water
½ teaspoon peppercorns
4 stalks celery
Blade of mace
8 slices carrot
1/3 cup Sherry
¾ onion sliced
½ teaspoon salt
1 small green pepper
1/8 teaspoon pepper

Put tomatoes and water in saucepan and add celery cut in pieces, carrot, onion, pepper (from which seeds have been removed), cloves, peppercorns and mace.
Bring to the boiling point and let simmer fifteen minutes.
Strain, and add sherry, salt, and pepper.
Cool and clear.
Serve in bouillon cups.

SOURCE: MRS FARMER, 1921

Mock Corn Bisque Soup

1 can corn
½ can tomatoes
1 quart milk
¼ teaspoon soda
1 slice onion
1/3 cup butter
3 tablespoons flour
2 teaspoons salt
¼ cup cold water
1/8 teaspoon pepper
1/8 teaspoon paprika

Scald milk in double boiler with corn and onion. Mix flour with cold water to form a smooth paste and add to scalded milk; then cook twenty minutes, stirring constantly at first and afterward occasionally, and rub through a sieve.

Cook tomatoes ten minutes, add soda, and rub through a sieve. Combine mixtures and strain into a tureen. Add butter bit by bit and seasonings.

SOURCE: MRS FARMER, 1921

Mock Hare Soup 1

2 Large Potatoes
1 Leek
1 Carrot
1 Stick of Celery
½ Turnip
5 oz Coarse Oatmeal
2 Cloves
1 ½ Pints of Stock or Water
½ oz Dripping
Salt and Pepper
1 teaspoonful of "meat essence" or cube

Chop the vegetables and put in a frying pan with the dripping and fry thoroughly. Add the oatmeal and cook until golden brown. Add the Salt and Pepper (to taste), cloves and stock and cook for half an hour on a low heat.

Sieve and add the meat essence or cube and then re-heat before serving. Serves 3 to 4 persons

SOURCE: ANON.

Mock Hare Soup II

1 litre Vegetable Stock
1 carrot (diced)
1 onion (diced)
1 stick of celery (diced)
1 tomato (diced)
2 cloves
1 bay leaf
1 tsp of chopped parsley
1 tbsp of flour
30 g of vegetable butter
salt
pepper

Melt the butter in a casserole, cut up the vegetables into neat pieces, and cook them slowly in the butter for about 15 minutes - with the lid on. Stir in the flour and brown it a little, then add the stock, cloves, bay leaf and seasoning, stir until it simmers; then cook gently for about 20 minutes.

Meanwhile make forcemeat balls about the size of a cherry, and fry them. Put them into the soup tureen, pour the soup on, scatter the chopped parsley over, and serve immediately.

Hand the red currant jelly separately. When in season a few mushrooms added to the vegetables are an improvement.

Notes
For forcemeat balls, see 'Mock Forcemeat' recipe
Time - About 45 minutes. Sufficient for about 6 or 7 persons

SOURCE MRS BEETON, 1861.

Mock Hare Soup III

1 lb Celery
1 lb Turnip
1 lb Carrot
1 lb Onion
1 lb Brown Lentils
2 oz. Butter
Jamaica Pepper and Salt to taste
3 quarts Water

Soak lentils for 24 hours. Cut down turnip, carrot and onions, and put into a pot with the butter. Toss and stir about in the pot over a brisk fire for about 15 minutes, but do not permit vegetables to brown. When boiling, put in lentils drained from the water in which they were soaked.

Boil soup slowly for 3 hours, then put through a hair sieve, rinse out pot, put soup back again into it, add ½ teaspoonful Jamaica pepper broken in a little water ; also salt to taste. Serve in hot tureen, with forcemeat balls or sippets of toast.

SOURCE: MRS E. W. KIRK, 1929

Mock Kidney Soup I

1 lb. Liver
2 Onions
2 tablespoonfuls Flour
1 tablespoonful Dripping
Salt and Pepper
Small Bone
Small bit of Carrot and Turnip.

Boil the bone with carrot and turnip in 9 breakfast-cupfuls water for 3 hours, then strain. Wash the liver thoroughly, dry it, and cut it up in very small bits. Chop up the onions. Put the dripping in a saucepan to melt and get quite hot.

Put in the onions, and fry them yellow, also fry. the liver till it looks a light colour; then add the flour, and mix well. Put all in saucepan till it looks brown, then add stock, 1 teaspoonful salt, and a little pepper and ketchup.

Stir well till it boils. Put on lid, and simmer for 2 hours. Add salt to taste, and serve.

SOURCE: MRS E. W. KIRK, 1929

Mock Kidney Soup II

Take ½ lb. liver, 1 onion, 1 oz. dripping, 2 pints bone stock, 1 mushroom, ½ carrot, ½ turnip, a little parsley, flour for thickening, seasoning.

Wash and cut up liver, fry onion (cut in rings) with the liver in the dripping until brown. Add to the stock and bring to the boll. Cut the vegetables Into small pieces and add.

Simmer for an hour, skimming frequently. Put all through a sieve. Stir the thickening (5 tablespoon flour to each pint of liquid) well in and boil for a few minutes.

Season to taste.

SECOND PRIZE, TWO FANCY LINEN TEA TOWELS, has been awarded to MISS M. WILSON, 8 Griver-street, Cottesloe, for MOCK DISHES.

SOURCE: SUNDAY TIMES 1934

Mock Lobster Bisque

Cook 1 quart of milk or white broth with 1 cup of shredded cod-fish in a double-boiler 20 minutes, then strain out the fish (use the fish in cream sauce on potatoes next morning).

Cook 2 cups of tomatoes, 2 slices of onion, a small piece of bay leaf, a few sprigs, each, of thyme and parsley 10 minutes; strain and add 1 teaspoonful of soda.

Melt 2 tablespoonfuls of butter; add 3 tablespoonfuls of flour and stir until well cooked, then let cool ; add a little of the hot milk, stir until smooth, then add the rest of the milk gradually and stir until boiling.

When ready to serve, combine the two mixtures. Serve in cups with a spoonful of whipped cream on the top of the soup in each cup. Season the cream with salt and paprika before whipping.

Note
Serves ten to twelve people

SOURCE: JANET MCKENZIE HILL ,1918

Mock Oyster Soup I

The oyster plant is used for this delicious dish - by many it is known as salsify. Scrape the vegetable and cut into small pieces with a silver knife (a steel knife would darken the oyster plant).

Cook in just enough water to keep from burning, and when tender press through a colander and return to the water in which it was cooked. Add three cups of hot milk which has been thickened with a little butter and flour and rubbed together and seasoned with salt and white pepper.

A little chopped parsley may be added before serving. cup cream instead of all milk greatly improves taste.

SOURCE: L. O. KLEBER 1915

A Note About Salsify

The vegetable called salsify is usually the root of purple salsify, Tragopogon porrifolius; the root is described as having the taste of oysters (hence the alternative common name "oyster plant" for some species in this genus), but more insipid with a touch of sweetness.

The young shoots of purple salsify can also be eaten, as well as young leaves.

Other species are also used in the same way, including the black or Spanish salsify, Scorzonera hispanica, which is closely related though not a member of the genus Tragopogon.

SOURCE: WIKIPEDIA

Mock Oyster Soup II

2 cups raw fish trimmings
sprig of parsley
1 small carrot, peeled and sliced
1 small turnip, peeled and sliced
6 white peppercorns
a little mace
seasoning
4 good roots of salsify, scraped and chopped into small pieces
4 tablespoons butter
1 level tablespoon flour
2 pints water
½ pint milk

Put raw fish trimmings in a saucepan with 2 pints of water. Add the parsley, carrot, turnip, mace and peppercorns. Simmer gently for 1 hour, then strain.

Put the salsify pieces in a saucepan with the strained stock and simmer for half an hour.

Melt the butter in another saucepan, sprinkle in the flour, and stir over a gentle heat until it becomes a smooth paste. Cook for 2 - 3 minutes.

Stir in gradually about a teacup of the soup into the paste. When quite smooth add this thickening to the soup and simmer for 5 minutes. Add seasoning to taste and ½ pint of hot milk.

Bring to the boil and serve.

SOURCE: ANON

Note - see 'Salsify', in Mock Oyster Soup I, above

3
MOCK MEATS & EGGS

Mock Black Pudding

1 cup oatmeal
1 pint vegetable or meat broth
salt, pepper
marjoram, thyme
2 - 3 small onions

Stew one cup of oatmeal in one pint of broth or vegetable water, add salt, pepper, marjoram, and thyme, simmer, stirring constantly until thickened.
Chop onions very fine, brown in little fat and stir in.

SOURCE: ANON

Notes

Black pudding, blood pudding or blood sausage is a type of sausage made by cooking blood or dried blood with a filler until it is thick enough to congeal when cooled. (Wikipedia)

Mock Brains I

Peel and thinly slice one onion, cook lightly in a little dripping in a saucepan, add 2 ½ cups boiling water, then add 1 cup rolled oats. Cook gently for 30 minutes, season with salt and pepper. Pour on to a plate, allow to cool, cut into portions.
Roll in egg and bread-crumbs, fry in smoking fat until brown, drain on crumpled brown paper.

SOURCE: CAIRNS POST, 1942

Mock Brains II

Cook 1 cup rolled oats in 1 ½ cups water with 1 cut-up onion and a teaspoon of butter. When very well cooked and thick season well with pepper and salt and put into a small basin to set. (If wanted for breakfast cook over night.)
When cold, cut in slices half an inch thick, dip in egg and bread-crumbs and fry a nice golden brown in plenty of boiling fat. Drain on paper and serve very hot, garnished with parsley.

SOURCE: EXAMINER, LAUNCESTON, 1947

Mock Brains: A thick porridge with onions, pepper and salt, fried to look like brains.

Mock Cutlets - Lentil

1 lb Lentils
1 large Onion
1 Beetroot
2 Eggs
1 tablespoon chopped Parsley,
1 teaspoon Thyme,
½ teacup Ketchup,
1 oz Butter,
Pepper and Salt.

Soak the lentils over-night; put them in a saucepan, with sufficient water to cover them, and stew gently till tender. Boil the beet root whole, and cut it in small pieces; chop the onion, and fry it.
Then mix all the ingredients together, and put them aside until quite cool; then mould into shapes the size of a cutlet; brush them with beaten egg; dip them in fine bread crumbs, and fry in boiling oil.

SOURCE: MRS E. W. KIRK, 1929

Mock Cutlets - Mushroom

2 lb tin mushrooms (minced fine)
2 well-beaten eggs
4 ounces of grated bread crumbs
Season with salt, pepper, and nutmeg.

Stir the whole smooth.
Mould into small flat cutlets; dip these in egg and bread crumbs;
fry in butter or hot vegetable oil till brown.

SOURCE: MRS E. W. KIRK, 1929

Mock Cutlets - Vegetable

1 tablespoon chopped parsley
1 tablespoon onion
1 tablespoon beetroot cooked and cut small
A little salt and pepper, ½ lb. wheaten bread crumbs
2 hard-boiled eggs, and a spoonful of butter.

Mix well together, and moisten with 2 eggs beaten; shape into cutlets, and fry.

SOURCE: MRS. E. W. KIRK, 1929

Mock Foie Gras

1 lb of calves' liver
½ lb of bacon
A small onion
1 teaspoonful of mignonette pepper
Mixed herbs
Parsley
1 oz of lard or bacon fat
1 teaspoonful of Bovril
1 large tablespoonful of very fine bread crumbs

Cut the liver into very small portions and cut up the bacon also, chop the onion and put all into a pan with the mixed herbs, pepper, chopped parsley and the hot lard or bacon fat ; stir over a quick fire for five or six minutes, then rub through a wire sieve whilst hot. Add the Bovril and bread crumbs and it is ready for use.

About Bovril

Bovril is the trademarked name of a thick, salty meat extract, developed in the 1870s by John Lawson Johnston and sold in a distinctive, bulbous jar. It is made in Burton upon Trent, Staffordshire, owned and distributed by Unilever UK.
Bovril can be made into a drink by diluting with hot water, or less commonly with milk. It can also be used as a flavouring for soups, stews or porridge, or spread on bread, especially toast. (Wikipedia)

SOURCE: CAIRNS POST 1928

Mock Forcemeat

6 Eggs
2 oz Butter
½ lb Bread Crumbs
½ oz Parsley
½ oz Beetroot
¼ o sweet Leeks
¼ oz. sweet Marjoram
Winter Savoury and Lemon Thyme mixed
3 tablespoonfuls Cream.

Boil 4 eggs hard; take out yolks, and mash them with the butter, adding herbs and bread crumbs; season with pepper and salt, and a little nutmeg. Add cream and 2 eggs (well-beaten); melt some butter in tin, and put in forcemeat, and roast before fire in Dutch oven. Serve with brown sauce, part of which may be poured on dish, and garnish with whites of eggs cut small.

About Forcemeat
Real forcemeat is a mixture of ground, lean meat emulsified with fat. (Wikipedia)

SOURCE: MRS E. W. KIRK, 1929

Mock Game

Cut some beefsteak into small squares, put a piece of bacon on each, roll up the beef, tie it or skewer it, dredge well with flour, and brown it in a saucepan containing a little hot dripping.
Add a little good stock and seasoning to taste, and stew gently till the meat is tender.
Arrange the meat on a hot dish, garnish with potatoes or sippets of toast, thicken the gravy, and pour over the meat. Serve at once.

SOURCE: AUSTRALIAN TOWN & COUNTRY JOURNAL, 1903

Mock Haggis

½ lb. of Flour
½ lb. of Bread Crumbs
6 oz. of Butter
a small Onion chopped
a small teacupful of Oatmeal
2 Eggs
Pepper and Salt to taste.
Mix together and moisten with water; Boil for about 3 hours.

SOURCE: MRS E. W. KIRK, 1929

About Haggis

Traditional haggis is a savoury pudding containing sheep's pluck (heart, liver and lungs); minced with onion, oatmeal, suet, spices, and salt, mixed with stock, and traditionally encased in the animal's stomach and simmered for approximately three hours.

SOURCE: WIKIPEDIA

Mock Hare

'Mock hare is delicious, and makes a nice change. '

2 lb. rump steak cut in thick pieces. Take a tablespoonful of olive oil and one of vinegar, mix and fry the meat in it rubbing the liquid in with a wooden spoon, then lay aside till the following forcemeat is prepared.

Take two cupfuls of bread-crumbs, one of finely chopped suet, one teaspoonful of salt half teaspoonful pepper, one dessert-spoonful dried herbs (thyme, mint parsley), and mix all together with a little milk.

Lay forcemeat on steak, roll up and skewer well, dredge with flour, place in a baking dish with some hot fat and bake one hour and a half, basting well.

Pour fat from tin when cooked, add tablespoonful flour, two tea-spoonfuls Bovril, hot water and salt to taste.

Bring gravy to the boil and pour over meat Serve at once.

SOURCE: SUNDAY TIMES, PERTH, 1912

About Bovril

Bovril is the trademarked name of a thick, salty meat extract, de-veloped in the 1870s by John Lawson Johnston and sold in a dis-tinctive, bulbous jar. It is made in Burton upon Trent, Stafford-shire, owned and distributed by Unilever UK.

Bovril can be made into a drink by diluting with hot water, or less commonly with milk. It can also be used as a flavouring for soups, stews or porridge, or spread on bread, especially toast.

SOURCE: WIKIPEDIA

Mock Meat Loaf

1 Tablespoon butter substitute
1 cup bread crumbs.
2 Tablespoon chopped onion
1 cup chopped nuts
Salt and pepper
1 cup cheese.
2 teaspoons lemon juice or vinegar

Cook onion in butter and a little water until tender. Mix all ingredients and add enough water to moisten. Pour into a shallow dish, and bake and brown.

SOURCE: MRS EDITH BLACKMAN, 1917

Mock Omelette

1 cup of chick pea flour
½ cup of finely chopped tomatoes
½ cup of finely chopped Onions
1 to 2 green chillies chopped finely
½ cup of any greens (Spinach, mint, coriander leaves)
salt to taste,
Water
Oil for cooking
Bread slices

Mix ingredients together with enough water to form a pancake consistency. Heat ½ teaspoon oil in a frying-pan or griddle and pour in a ladle full of the mixture.

With the ladle, shape it into a disk about the size of a crepe. Keep it on medium low heat, and cover with a lid.

Let it cook for about three minutes, remove lid and spread about ½ teaspoon of oil.

Slowly flip the omelette to cook the other side. When cooked remove and keep it warm until it is served.

SOURCE: ANON

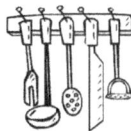

Mock Omelette - Savoury

One slice day-old bread 1 inch thick
5 tablespoons boiling milk
1 egg
1 dessertspoon chopped parsley
Salt and pepper to taste
1 oz. butter or substitute

Place bread (crusts removed) in basin, add milk, stand 10 minutes.
Add egg, beat until mixture is smooth. Fold in parsley, salt
and pepper.
Prepare omelet pan, using half the shortening.
Place remaining shortening in pan, melt, pour in mixture. Cook
over gentle heat until set and browned underneath.
Brown top under griller. Place on heated serving-dish, spoon fill-
ing along one side, fold over.

Kidney and Onion Filling:

Melt l oz. butter or substitute in pan, add 1 tablespoon chopped
onion and 1 sheep's kidney (previously skinned and diced).
Fry until lightly brown.
Add 1 dessertspoon flour, brown, and cook 2 to 3 minutes.
Add 1 cup stock, stir until boiling. Season.

Brains and Corn Filling:

Mix together 1 set chopped cooked brains, 1 dessertspoon chopped
cooked bacon, ½ cup tinned corn, 1 cup medium thickness white
sauce.
Season to taste, reheat.

SOURCE: ANON.

Mock Pork

'Second prize, two fancy linen tea towels, has been awarded to Miss M. Wilson, 8 Griyer-street, Cottesloe, for mock dishes. '

Soak half a pound of haricot beans overnight.
Chop finely two large onions, put beans and onions into a saucepan, just cover with water and simmer slowly. When soft, turn into a basin and mash.
Add 2 oz. butter or margarine, ¼ lb. bread-crumbs, a dash of pepper, salt and a little sage. Bind with a well-beaten egg and half teacup of milk. Make into a thick roll.
Put into a baking tin with some dripping, baste well and bake to a nice brown. Serve with apple sauce.

SOURCE: SUNDAY TIMES, PERTH,1934

Mock Sausages - Wartime

White cabbage
1 pound of boiled potatoes
1 cup breadcrumbs
salt, pepper
caraway seeds

Soft-boil the white cabbage and put through mincer together with boiled potatoes, add salt, pepper, caraway, and breadcrumbs
Mix well, shape into small sausages, and fry in little fat.

SOURCE: ANON.

Mock Sausages with Fried Apple Rings

Pick over one-half cup Lima beans and soak overnight in cold water to cover. Drain and cook in boiling, salted water until soft;- again drain and force through a puree strainer; there should be three-fourths cup pulp.

Add one-third cup rolled dried bread crumbs, three tablespoons heavy cream or butter, a few grains pepper, one-fourth teaspoon salt, one-half teaspoon sage, and one egg beaten slightly.

Shape in the form of sausages, dip in crumbs, egg and crumbs, and fry in olive oil. Drain, arrange on serving dish and garnish with fried apple rings.

SOURCE: MRS FARMER 1921

Mock Sausages - Mrs Kirk

Boil 3 carrots, 4 onions, and 2 parsnips. Then chop all fine and prepare ½ pint of yellow peas, cook them soft; pound them well up; add the chopped vegetables, also layer chopped parsley, a small bit of garlic chopped, salt and pepper, with 2 eggs and ½ lb. bread crumbs to stiffen the whole.

Roll into pieces about size of ordinary sausages; dip in egg and bread crumbs; then fry in butter or vegetable oil. The oil must be boiling.

SOURCE: MRS E. W. KIRK, 1929

Mock Sausages - Australian

'"ROEITA" wins the first prize this week with these recipes.'

Boil 1 cup of rolled oats in ¾ cup of salted water for 15 minutes, then add finely chopped onion for flavour.
Mix well and empty into a basin.
When cool, add 1 beaten egg, pepper and herbs to taste, 1 cup bread-crumbs. Shape into sausages, roll in flour and fry in deep boiling fat until golden brown.
Very tasty and a good substitute for meat.

SOURCE: THE CENTRAL QUEENSLAND HERALD, 1943

Mock Steak

Bread is cut about ¼ inch thick into any shape preferred, the crust being removed. The pieces are first dipped in milk, not soaked, and then in beaten egg, and fried with butter until brown. The beaten egg may be flavoured with parsley, thyme, or other herb.
Another variation is the use of ketchup diluted with water, instead of milk, in which to dip the bread. This gives a savoury omelet.

Pieces of bread may also be prepared as above, then rolled in bread crumbs and fried in boiling fat. Dish in a ring, with fried onions, tomatoes, or mushrooms in the centre.

SOURCE: MRS. E. W. KIRK, 1929

Mock Sweetbreads - Mrs Farmer

Finely chop one-pound lean veal, add two ounces finely chopped fat salt pork, and work, using the hands, until well blended; then add two-thirds cup soft bread crumbs, two eggs, slightly beaten, one-third cup flour, one-half cup rich milk, one-half teaspoon salt and one-eighth teaspoon pepper. Form into eight elliptical-shaped pieces, put in dish, dot over with butter, using one and one-half tablespoons, and pour around three-fourths cup chicken stock.
Cover and bake one hour, basting every ten minutes of the cooking. Remove to hot serving dish and pour around white, brown or tomato sauce.

SOURCE: MRS FARMER, 1921

Mock Sweetbreads - Mrs Kirk

Stew 1 large parsnip, 1 onion, and 1 artichoke in milk, and flavour with white pepper, very little salt, and a small pinch mace.
When quite soft, cut parsnip in slices and place on top of each piece of Cheddar cheese of same size. Lay these on a thick slice of buttered toast and put in quick oven till cheese becomes soft and slightly brown.
While this is cooking, thicken the milk after straining onion and artichoke from it, with a nut of butter and a small spoonful flour. When the sauce boils 5 minutes, pour it on the "sweetbreads" when they are taken from the oven.
Decorate with small sprigs of parsley.

SOURCE: MRS E. W. KIRK, 1929

Mock Rabbit I

1 ½ cups cold cooked chicken or veal, cut in dice
Whites 2 "hard-boiled" eggs, chopped
1 cup White Sauce I (see below)
3 tablespoons Sherry wine
Yolks 2 "hard-boiled" eggs, finely chopped
¼ teaspoon salt
Few grains cayenne

Add to sauce chicken, yolks and whites of eggs, salt, and cayenne; cook two minutes, and add wine.

White Sauce I
2 tablespoons butter
1 cup milk
2 tablespoons flour
¼ teaspoon salt
Few grains pepper

Put butter in saucepan, stir until melted and bubbling; add flour mixed with seasonings, and stir until thoroughly blended; then pour on gradually while stirring constantly the milk, bring to the boiling-point and let boil two minutes. If a wire whisk is used, all the milk may be added at once.

SOURCE: MRS FARMER, 1918.

Mock Rabbit II

Have ready cooked half a calf's liver (it may be boiled or braised with vegetables).

Cut it into small cubes. Put one-fourth a cup of butter into the blazer; when coloured a little add the cubes of liver dredged with two tablespoonfuls of flour, one-fourth a teaspoonful of paprika and half a teaspoonful of salt.

Stir and cook until the flour is blended with the butter; then add one cup of water or stock and one teaspoonful of chopped parsley. As soon as the sauce boils, add one-fourth a cup of cream, two hard-boiled eggs chopped fine, and one teaspoonful of lemon juice. Serve on toast, with quarters of lemon cut lengthwise.

SOURCE: JANET MCKENZIE HILL, 1909

Note: Cream may be used in the place of stock, and the yolks of two uncooked eggs instead of the cooked eggs.

Mock Toad-in-the-Hole

A quarter of a pound of cooked lentils
A quarter of a pound of mashed potatoes
A teaspoonful of mixed herbs
Half an egg
Half a teaspoonful each of salt and pepper
Half an ounce of butter
Batter

Have prepared a batter. Chop lentils, then, add potatoes, herbs, salt and pepper. Shape into six sausages, and fry until brown; put them in a greased tin, and pour the batter over; bake for thirty minutes in a moderate oven.

SOURCE: ELTHAM AND WHITTLESEA SHIRES ADVER-TISER AND DIAMOND CREEK VALLEY ADVOCATE, 1918

Mock Venison I

This may be made with fresh meat, or as a réchauffé of cold mutton.

If the former, bone a piece of well-hung loin of mutton, and stew the bones in stock very gently for two hours with an onion, a carrot, sweet herbs, a stick of celery, and one or two cloves and peppercorns.

Strain the soup, return it to the pan, place the mutton in it, and simmer until the meat is tender.

Remove the meat, and brown it in a hot oven.

Strain the gravy, thicken it, and season to taste; add a little browning and port- wine.

Dish the meat on a hot dish, surround with the gravy, and serve very hot, with red currant jelly or any sharp preserve.

If cold cooked mutton be used, it must be cut in thick slices, and simmered in the same way.

The stock may be made of a little water, finely-chopped onion, a glass of claret or port, a tablespoonful of red-currant jelly, a little glaze, and a tablespoonful of chutney.

SOURCE: AUSTRALIAN TOWN & COUNTRY JOURNAL, 1903

Mock Venison II

Bone a loin of well-hung mutton, skin it, and set in a stewpan with 1 ½ pints of water, an onion stuck thickly with cloves, and a dessert spoonful of tarragon vinegar.
When all this boils up, skim, add a bouquet of mixed thyme and parsley, with a nice seasoning of pepper and salt.
Stew for two hours, turning constantly.
Add, at intervals, some gravy made from the bones.
When the mock venison is nearly done, put it in a roaster, and brown in a sharp oven. Serve with rich brown gravy, in which both red currant jelly and port wine are blended.

SOURCE: WESTERN MAIL, PERTH, 1903

#

Mock Venison Pasty

Stew an ox cheek for an hour and a half in some good stock; add vegetables and herbs; when quite tender remove the meat from the bones of the cheek and cut it in slices.
Line a dish with puff paste down the sides, and lay the slices in the dish, then strain the gravy and again put it in the stewpan flavouring it with ketchup and half a tea-cupful of port wine.
Pour it over the cheek, cover with paste and bake.
Should the meat be stewed in weak broth or water, some good gravy must be added to it afterwards.
If carefully made, it is little inferior to a real venison pasty.

SOURCE: JH WALSH 1859

Mock Venison Steak

Take a thick slice from a leg of mutton, a tablespoonful of vinegar, one of ketchup, the juice of a lemon, a few strips of the rind, a small onion, four cloves, a little extract of meat, an ounce of flour, an ounce of butter, a tablespoonful of red-currant jelly.

Put the steak on a dish with the vinegar, ketchup, the juice of half the lemon, the onion cut in rings, the cloves, a few strips of lemon-peel, and leave it to soak for twenty-four hours.

Grease the bottom of à saucepan, put in the steak and seasoning, and enough water to cover it, and a teaspoonful of meat extract.

Simmer very gently for about two hours; put the steak on a hot dish, thicken the gravy with the butter and flour, boil up; add the rest of the lemon-juice, pepper and salt, and the currant jelly. Pour over the steak and serve.

SOURCE: AUSTRALIAN TOWN & COUNTRY JOURNAL, 1900

Mock Venison - Stewed

Take a fat loin of mutton, the outer skin must be stripped off and the bones cut out.

Put the bones into a stewpan with a good-sized onion stuck with cloves, one anchovy, some peppercorns and a bunch of sweet herbs. Stew for three hours in a small quantity of water, then strain. The mutton should be beaten with a rolling-pin, and nutmeg grated over the inside the previous night.

Before it is put in the stewpan it must be rolled up tight, beginning at the tail end, and tied with a strong string. Add half a pint of port-wine to the gravy, and let it all stew together for three hours at least. A large loin or saddle will require four hours. When done the fat must be skimmed off, and the gravy thickened with a little flour and butter, and a small quantity of ketchup added.

SOURCE: JH WALSH, 1859

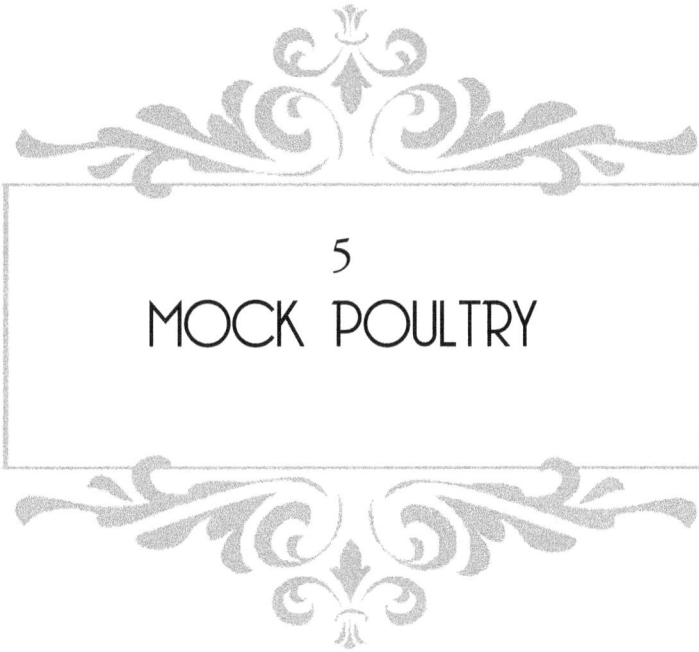

5
MOCK POULTRY

Mock Chicken I

Procure a young and fresh rabbit, soak it for 1 hour in strong salt and water. Cut it into dainty portions; lay it nicely in a large pan, cover it with milk and a little water, season with pepper and salt.
Lay a large stick of celery (well washed and cut daintily) in top; do not stir or move.
Simmer very gently, never boiling, for quite a long time.
When the rabbit is tender (from 1 ½ to 2 hours) pour out liquid and thicken with plain flour, and add finely chopped parsley.
Serve the rabbit and celery very neatly, and pour the sauce over it

SOURCE: BARRIER MINER, BROKEN HILL, NSW 1926

Mock Chicken II

1 tablespoon each of butter, onion, grated cheese.
1 tomato, herbs, 1 egg, salt and pepper. Mix.

SOURCE: ANON

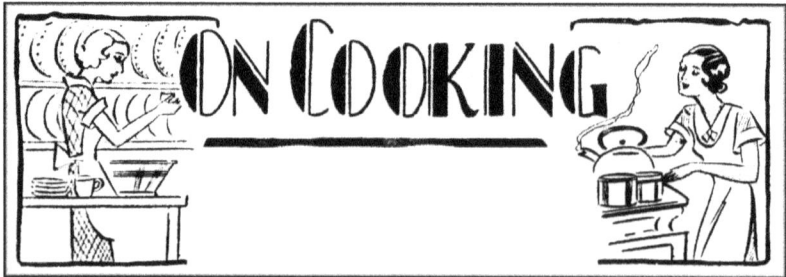

Mock Chicken III

1 tablespoon butter
2 medium onions, chopped
2 tomatoes, diced
1 egg, lightly beaten
1-2 teaspoons mixed herbs
Salt and pepper, to taste
1½ cups grated tasty cheese

Melt butter in pan. Add onion and cook until soft and golden.
Add tomatoes and cook until moisture evaporates.
Add egg and stir until scrambled. Stir in herbs, salt and pepper.
Remove from heat and stir in cheese until melted.
Delicious on toast

SOURCE: ANON

Mock Chicken IV

1 white onion chopped finely
1 tomato chopped finely
1 egg, well-beaten
Pinch of mixed herbs
Butter or Oil for cooking
Slices of bread

Simmer onion in saucepan with butter or oil, until soft. Add to-mato, stir until cooked. Add egg.
Cook for a few minutes, add salt and pepper and mixed herbs to taste.
Lightly grill the back side of the bread pieces.
Spread mixture onto each slice of bread and place back under the griller to brown.

SOURCE: ANON

Mock Chicken Pie

Take as many potatoes as desired for six persons, 9 eggs, 1 salt-spoon of salt and of sage, 1 lb. of pastry, 4 small onions, pepper to taste, 1 table spoon of butter.

Halve the potatoes, but leave the onions whole.

Beat two of the eggs well and add seasoning and enough cold water to cover the potatoes.

Boil gently till the vegetables are tender, then place in casserole dish, drop in the other eggs, broken whole, cover with pastry, and bake about 20 minutes.

SOURCE: ADVOCATE, TASMANIA 1934

Mock Duck I

1 flank steak
1 teaspoon salt
1 teaspoon pepper
1 teaspoon Worcestershire sauce
1 cup breadcrumbs
1 tablespoon onion juice
1 tablespoon chopped parsley
½ teaspoon poultry seasoning
1 pint boiling water
1/3 cup of whole wheat flour

Reserve the water and the flour.
Mix other ingredients. Spread on steak.
Roll the steak and tie.
Roll in the flour. Brown in two tablespoons of fat.
Add the water. Cover and cook until tender.

SOURCE: GOUDISS 1918

Mock Duck II

Take a piece of beefsteak, about 10 in or 12 in in extent, and spread
it with a layer of sage and onion stuffing, roll up the steak, tie it in
shape, put it in a deep dish, with half a pint of good stock or gravy,
and bake for about an hour, turning and basting it frequently.
Remove the string, put the meat on a hot dish, thicken the gravy,
pour it round the meat, and serve.

SOURCE: AUSTRALIAN TOWN & COUNTRY JOURNAL
1903

Mock Duck III

Select a nice piece of steak, spread it out and spread a little butter over with the point of a knife; now sprinkle lightly with pepper and salt.

Take one and a-half cups of bread crumbs, one onion chopped fine: take two ripe tomatoes, dip in hot water, and skin them; mash with fork, and mix with bread crumbs and onion, which should previously be sprinkled with pepper and salt.

Place all in steak and roll, tie round with string; put in hot dish of fat: bake steadily for one hour.

SOURCE: MORNING BULLETIN, QUEENSLAND 1907

Mock Duck IV

Fry one medium diced onion in good ounce butter. Add one large peeled tomato, ½ teaspoon or more salt, ½ teaspoon herbs, one large well beaten egg.

Delicious spread on toast or used as a sandwich filling.

SOURCE: ANON

Mock Roast Duck

1 Large Vegetable Marrow
2 large Onions
1 teaspoonful of Sage,
a breakfast-cupful soaked Bread
1 oz of Butter
1 Egg
Pepper and Salt to taste.

Trim the marrow, cut in halves lengthwise, take out the seeds; parboil the onion, and chop it fine; mix it with the bread, sage, butter, pepper, and salt. Fill the marrow with the mixture, put both halves together; brush butter over them, and bake ½ hour. This is excellent; some vegetarians call it "vegetable roast duck."

SOURCE: KIRK, 1929

Mock Goose

1 liver
½ lb Bacon
2 onions
Pepper and salt
7 potatoes
1 cup water or stock
1 tablespoon flour
1 oz Dripping
1 teaspoon powdered sage.

Soak liver in salt and water. Cut into slices and dry on cloth.
Cut up bacon, potatoes and onions. Dip liver in flour. Put in layers
in pie-dish, finishing with vegetable layer. Pour water or stock over
all. Bake 1 ½ -2 hours.

SOURCE: ADVOCATE, TASMANIA 1945

Mock Goose

1 ½ lb Potatoes
2 large cooking apples
4 oz cheese
Half a teaspoon dried sage
Salt and pepper
Three quarters of a pint vegetable stock
1 tablespoon flour

Scrub and slice potatoes thinly, slice apples, grate cheese.

Grease a fireproof dish, place a layer of potatoes on it, cover with apples and a little sage, season lightly and sprinkle with cheese, repeat layers leaving potatoes and cheese to cover.

Pour in half a pint of the stock and cook in a moderate oven for three quarters of an hour. Blend flour with remainder of the stock, pour into dish and cook for another quarter hour.

Serve as a main dish with a green vegetable.

Quantity: 4 helpings

SOURCE: ANON

Mock Goose III

In a deep pie-dish put a few small lumps of dripping; then a layer of sliced apples sprinkled slightly with sugar; a layer of sage and onion stuffing; then some slices of liver; and next a layer of raw potatoes sprinkled with salt.

If the family is a large one repeat the layers, but be sure to end up with the layer of potatoes.

On top dot some pieces of dripping. Bake for an hour in a moderate oven. Serve very hot.

'Second prize, two fancy linen tea towels, has been awarded to Miss M. Wilson, 8 Griyer-street, Cottesloe, for Mock Dishes. '

SOURCE: SUNDAY TIMES, PERTH, 1934

Mock Goose Pudding

¼ lb. scraps of Bread
Tablespoonful Flour
Pinch of Pepper and Salt
Lump of Dripping the size of an egg
Teaspoonful Sage rubbed down
2 tablespoonfuls Milk.

Soak bread with boiling water, and drain well; add dry ingredients, then milk.

Place mixture in well-greased tin; shred the dripping over the top, and bake 20 minutes.

Cut in squares, and serve hot or cold.

SOURCE: KIRK, 1929

Mock Goose with Stuffing

150 g (6 oz) cup dried lentils
½ pint water
A little lemon juice
Salt and pepper to taste
For the stuffing -
Breadcrumbs (made from two slices),
Chopped onion
Fresh sage

Simmer the lentils until all the water has been absorbed. Add lemon juice and season. Then to make the stuffing fry the onion in a little water, drain and add breadcrumbs and chopped sage. Place half the lentil mixture in an ovenproof dish, then layer on the stuffing and top with the remaining lentils. Cook at 180 C (356 F) until crisp.
Accompany with boiled potatoes and shredded cabbage cooked in a modicum of water. Reserve the cooking liquor to make gravy.

SOURCE: THE MINISTRY OF FOOD (UK), 1939-1945

Mock Pigeons

Take a piece of fillet of veal, and cut it into pieces, about the size of half a pigeon. Make a little forcemeat, and add to it some grated or minced ham.
Spread each piece of veal with a little of the forcemeat, roll it up, tie it with tape, and stew in good stock for three-quarters of an hour.
Place the meat in a tin, butter it, dust with flour, and bake for a few minutes in a hot oven.
Arrange on a hot dish, remove the tapes, pour some thick brown gravy round, garnish with sippets of toast, and serve with bread sauce.

SOURCE: AUSTRALIAN TOWN & COUNTRY JOURNAL, 1903

Note: See "Mock Forcemeat" recipe in this book.

Mock Pigeons II

3 or 4 fillets of veal,
Force-meat of bread-crumbs and minced pork, seasoned
½ cup mushrooms and a little minced onion.
1 sweetbread
A dozen oysters
½ cup strong brown gravy
1 glass of wine

Take the bone, if there be any, out of the fillets (or cutlets, or steaks) of veal; spread each thickly with the force-meat, and roll up tightly, binding with pack-thread.

Put into a baking-pan with enough cold water to half-cover them; turn another pan over them and bake from three-quarters of an hour to an hour in pro portion to their size. Meanwhile, boil the sweetbread fifteen minutes, blanch in cold water; cut into dice, and put into a saucepan with the gravy, which let simmer on the hob. Cut the mushrooms into small pieces and fry with the onion in a little butter, then add to the heating gravy. In still another vessel, when the veal is nearly done, heat the oysters, also chopped fine, seasoning with salt and pepper. When the "pigeons" are tender throughout, uncover, baste generously with butter, and brown. Transfer to a hot flat dish; clip the pack-thread and gently withdraw it, not to injure the shape of the rolled meat. Let the gravy in which they were roasted come to a fast boil, thicken with browned flour and pour into the saucepan containing the sauce, sweetbreads, etc. Boil up once, add the wine; take from the fire and put in the chopped oysters. Stir all together well in the saucepan, pour a dozen spoonfuls, or so, over the "pigeons," taking up the thickest part; send the rest to table in a gravy tureen. You can make a simpler sauce by leaving out the sweetbreads, etc., and seasoning the gravy in the baking-pan with tomato sauce. These "pigeons" will make an attractive variety in the home bill of fare, and do well as the piece de resistance of a family dinner.

SOURCE: HARLAND 1875

Mock Pigeons III

'Mrs A. H. Pickard, 35 May St, Deepdene, sent in this recipe, which wins for her 5/ worth of war savings stamps. The lemon rind gives this dish a delicious flavour.'

Take 2 slices of veal (1 coupon). Flatten out and spread with a seasoning of damped breadcrumbs, thyme, finely chopped parsley, and a little chopped lemon rind.
Roll the meat up and bind into oblong rolls.
Lay in a deep dish, and pour over some stock of gravy.
Cover dish, and bake in a moderate oven for about two hours, basting the meat occasionally.
To brown nicely remove the lid for the last 15 minutes.
When cooked take out the gravy and thicken with flour and season with pepper, salt, and ketchup.
Boil up again and pour some of the gravy over the mock pigeons and serve the rest in a gravy boat.

SOURCE: THE ARGUS, MELBOURNE 1944

Mock Turkey I

Perhaps you are going to be sternly frugal, and send to your Christmas table, mock duck, mock goose, or mock turkey. Every cook has her own pet scheme of - what shall we name it - deception?

One will procure a portion of steak, spread it with a stuffing of sago and onions, roll it, tie or skewer it, roast it, and send it to table, accompanied by green peas and apple sauce, under the pseudonym of "mock duck." Another will have a leg of mutton "boned" at the butchers, and will stuff it with sausage meat stuffing, give it an accompaniment of ham and bread sauce, and honour it with the name "Mock Turkey."

One receipt Penelope stumbled across not long since and tried with brilliant success evolved a tender (but meatless) mock turkey. Here it is for others to try:

"Put three cups of breadcrumbs into a bowl, and cover with hot cream. Mix thoroughly, and when cold add three well-beaten eggs and three cups of cold boiled rice. Be sure the rice is dry and the grains quite separate.

Next add three hard-boiled eggs, minced finely, and three cups of walnuts, which, have been skinned and put through a nut mill or meat chopper.

Mix in two tablespoons of chopped celery tops or dried celery, one tablespoon of chopped onion or half-teaspoonful of grated nutmeg, and salt to taste. Mix thoroughly, and then shape as much like the body of a turkey as possible.

Take two tablespoonsful of the mixture and form the thigh.
Put a skewer half-way in the thigh, then fasten to the body. One
tablespoonful is formed into the wing.

Brush with beaten eggs, and sprinkle with breadcrumbs. Put into a
greased baking dish and set in a hot oven.

As soon as it begins to bake, baste with a mixture of hot water,
butter, and salt, using one cup of water, one tablespoonful of butter, and half a teaspoonful of salt.

Baste about four times."

This turkey. Penelope may state, requires the most careful manipu-
lation in removing it from the baking dish to the china dish. It
should be served with bread sauce and ham, and is as good made
with Brazilian nuts as with walnuts, or very nearly.

SOURCE: THE SYDNEY MORNING HERALD 1917

Mock Turkey II

1 lb Lentils
Egg
Bread Crumbs
Butter
Parsley
Salt

Boil thoroughly 1 lb lentils (or half peas and lentils) in a cloth with a little salt.
Oil an enamelled dish, and line bottom and sides with the lentils.
Prepare a stuffing of bread crumbs, parsley, eggs, &c., the same as for turkey.
Fill up the dish with the stuffing, and cover with the rest of the lentils.
Put a few pieces of butter on the top, and bake 45 minutes to an hour.
Serve hot.

SOURCE: KIRK 1929

6
MOCK SEAFOOD

Mock Anchovies

When sprats are cheap, buy a good quantity, what in England you would call a peck. Do not either wipe or wash them.

Take four ounces of saltpetre, a pound of bay salt, two pounds of common coarse salt, and pound them well, then add a little cochineal to colour it, pound and mix very well.

Take a stone jar and put in it a layer of the mixture and a layer of the sprats, on each layer of fish adding three or four bay leaves and a few whole pepper-corns.

Fill up the jar and press it all down very firmly. Cover with a stone cover, and let them stand for six months before you use them.

SOURCE: LUCK 1915

Mock Caviar I

This is another lost wartime recipe. Having been unable to find the original we've had to replace it with a modern one.

    12 ozs chopped black olives
    8 ozs diced green peppers
    14 ½ ozs diced tomatoes
    3 chopped green onions
    2 cloves chopped garlic
    1 tbsp olive oil
    2 tsps red wine vinegar
    1 tsp ground black pepper
    1 pinch salt

Mix all ingredients, cover, and chill overnight. Serve this dip cold or at room temperature.

SOURCE: ANON

Mock Caviar II

1 ½ cups olives ripe, finely chopped
1 tablespoon anchovies chopped
1 teaspoon vegetable oil
2 teaspoons lemon juice
1 tablespoon scallions, spring or green onions thinly sliced
2 large eggs hard boiled, finely chopped

Mix all ingredients, cover, and chill overnight. Serve this dip cold or at room temperature.

SOURCE: ANON

Mock Crab I

Break up half a pound of soft, rich cheese with a fork, mix with it a teaspoonful of dry mustard, a saltspoonful of salt, half a salt-spoonful of pepper, and a dessertspoonful of vinegar; serve it cold, with a plate of thin bread and butter, or crisp crackers.

SOURCE: CORSON, 1877

Mock Crab II

3 hard-boiled egg whites, chopped
1 tablespoon grated cheese
2 teaspoons mustard sauce
1 tablespoon sugar
1 tablespoon grated raw onion
Tomato puree
salt

Mix together the first five ingredients. Add tomato puree bit by bit until dish has the consistency of real crabmeat. Add salt to taste.

SOURCE: ANON

Mock Crab III

4 tablespoonsful butter
1 ½ cupsful milk
½ cupful flour
1 can of corn
1 ½ teaspoonsful salt
8 teaspoonsful Worcestershire sauce
¾ Teaspoonful mustard
1 cup cracker crumbs
¼ teaspoonful paprika

Melt butter, add flour mixed with dry seasonings and pour on gradually the milk. Add corn, egg slightly beaten and Worcestershire sauce. Pour into a buttered baking dish, cover with crumbs and bake until top is brown.

This is a well flavoured corn dish, tasting so nearly like devilled crab that one can hardly detect the difference. Served with potatoes and a crisp green salad, it is an ideal combination. The recipe makes enough to serve four or five persons, at a cost of about 85 cents.

SOURCE: NEW-YORK TRIBUNE 1920

Mock Crabs

4 tablespoons butter
1½ cups scalded milk
½ cup flour
1 can Kornlet
1½ teaspoons salt
1 egg
¾ teaspoon mustard
3 teaspoons Worcestershire Sauce
¼ teaspoon paprika
1 cup buttered cracker crumbs

Melt butter, add flour mixed with dry seasonings, and pour on gradually the milk. Add Kornlet, egg slightly beaten, and Worcestershire Sauce. Pour into a buttered baking-dish, cover with crumbs, and bake until crumbs are brown.

SOURCE: FARMER 1918.

About Kornlet
Kornlet is a canned extract of green corn.

Mock Crab Toast

Melt a tablespoonful of butter in the blazer, turning it about so as to butter the surface thoroughly.

Put in half a pound of mild cheese, grated, and stir until the cheese is melted; then add the yolks of three eggs, beaten and diluted with a tablespoonful of anchovy sauce, a teaspoonful of made mustard, two tablespoonfuls of lemon juice or vinegar and one-fourth a teaspoonful of paprika.

Stir until smooth. Serve upon the untoasted side of sippets of bread toasted on one side.

SOURCE: MCKENZIE HILL, 1909

Mock Fish

4 potatoes, grated
1 tablespoon flour
2 eggs
Salt and pepper

Soak excess liquid from potatoes with paper towel and place in a bowl. Add flour, eggs, salt and pepper.

Heat oil in a pan. Form potato mixture into patties and cook until browned.

SOURCE: ANON

Mock Fish Patties

1 cup macaroni
¾ cup milk
4 tbsp plain flour
75 grams diced brown onion
50 grams chopped tasty cheddar cheese
2 cloves crushed garlic
1 tsp salt
1 chopped boiled egg
1 egg beaten
Breadcrumbs for coating

Boil the macaroni in water for 10 minutes. Drain.
Put the flour, milk, onion, cheese, garlic and salt in a saucepan to make the sauce. Whisk over medium heat till combined.
Remove from the heat and add drained macaroni and chopped egg. Flatten into an oiled round pie dish. Place in the refrigerator to set. When set cut into triangles.
Roll in the beaten egg and some breadcrumbs. Fry in a small amount of heated olive oil. an be eaten cold or warm.

SOURCE: ANON

Mock Lobster

1-½ to 2 pounds cod or haddock
1-½ teaspoons salt
2 teaspoons paprika
3 tablespoons white vinegar

Cut fillets into bite sized pieces (approximately 2 inches x 2 inches)
and put them in a deep frying-pan.
Cover with cold water.
Add salt and paprika, and bring the water to the boil.
Reduce heat and simmer, uncovered, for ten minutes. Drain.
Cover with cold water again. Add vinegar and bring to a boil for a
second time.
As before, reduce heat and simmer, uncovered, for ten minutes or
until you can easily break the fish into flakes with a fork.
Drain the mock lobster and serve it hot with melted butter and
lemon wedges.

SOURCE: ANON

Mock Oysters I

Take as many artichokes as will fill a dish, season with salt and pepper. Boil in milk until tender.
Take a small tin of sardines, free from oil, mash all well together,
put in a pie dish, place breadcrumbs on top, and also a few dots
of butter.
Brown in a moderate oven.

SOURCE: ADVOCATE, TASMANIA 1929

Mock Oysters II

Boil oyster-plant till soft, mash through a sieve, beat eggs light, allowing one egg to one teacup of vegetable. Form into balls with floured hands, and sauté brown.

SOURCE: MILLET BAXTER, 1913

About Salsify

The vegetable called salsify is usually the root of purple salsify, Tragopogon porrifolius; the root is described as having the taste of oysters (hence the alternative common name "oyster plant" for some species in this genus), but more insipid with a touch of sweetness. The young shoots of purple salsify can also be eaten, as well as young leaves. Other species are also used in the same way, including the black or Spanish salsify, Scorzonera hispanica, which is closely related though not a member of the genus Tragopogon

SOURCE: WIKIPEDIA

Mock Oysters III

To one cup of Kornlet add two well-beaten eggs, two tablespoonfuls of flour, a scant half teaspoonful of salt and a dash of paprika. Drop, by spoonfuls, into a hot, well-oiled blazer and cook to a golden brown, turn, and brown the other side.
Kornlet is a canned extract of green corn.

SOURCE: MCKENZIE HILL, 1909

Mock Oysters IV

To one can of Kornlet add a teaspoonful of soda, two well-beaten eggs, salt and pepper, and enough fine cracker crumbs to hold the mixture together. Drop from a spoon and cook as above.
Kornlet is a canned extract of green corn.

SOURCE: MCKENZIE HILL, 1909

Mock Oysters V

To one pint of green corn pulp add salt and pepper to taste, two well-beaten eggs, and flour enough to hold the pulp together. Sauté by spoonfuls in frying-pan, first on one side and then the other. Serve hot.
Kornlet is a canned extract of green corn.

SOURCE: BAXTER, 1913

Mock Fried Oysters

Fried green tomatoes have a flavor that is considered like fried oysters and are very tasty served with bacon or chops, steak, etc.
Select tomatoes that show no sign of ripening (just green), cut them in two and pour boiling water over them.
Set on side of stove to keep warm (not boil) for about 10 or 15 minutes, then drain and dry with a cloth.
Dip slices in a beaten egg then in fine oatmeal or cornmeal, and fry in boiling hot bacon fat or butter if preferred, and serve hot with the morning bacon.
Apples sliced and done the same are nice with bacon.

SOURCE: SUNDAY TIMES, PERTH, 1935

Mock Oyster Sandwiches

Skin, and cook 2 sets of brains with a small piece of onion, 2 bay leaves, salt, and cayenne.
Cool and chop up roughly. Stir in very carefully 1 teaspoon anchovy sauce, 1 dessert spoon cream, and a squeeze of lemon juice. Prepare carefully so that the mixture will not be too moist and soft for spreading.

SOURCE: THE CHARLEVILLE TIMES, 1941

Mock Oyster Stew

One bunch oyster plant, eight teaspoonfuls butter, a little flour or corn starch, vinegar and water for boiling, pepper and salt, one-half cup of milk.

Wash and scrape the oyster plant very carefully; drop into weak vinegar and water, bring quickly to a boil, and cook ten minutes; turn off the vinegar water, and rinse the salsify in boiling water; throw this out, and cover with more from the tea kettle; stew gently ten minutes longer; add pepper and salt and two tablespoonfuls of butter; stew in this until tender.

Meanwhile beat, in a farina kettle, the milk; thicken, add the remaining butter, and keep dry until the salsify is done, then transfer it to this sauce; pepper and salt; let all lie together in the inner kettle, the water in the outer at a slow boil, for five minutes; pour into a covered dish.

SOURCE: WILLEY, 1884

About Salsify

The vegetable called salsify is usually the root of purple salsify, Tragopogon porrifolius; the root is described as having the taste of oysters (hence the alternative common name "oyster plant" for some species in this genus), but more insipid with a touch of sweetness. The young shoots of purple salsify can also be eaten, as well as young leaves. Other species are also used in the same way, including the black or Spanish salsify, Scorzonera hispanica, which is closely related though not a member of the genus Tragopogon

SOURCE: WIKIPEDIA

Mock Whitebait

Fillet a bream, and cut it into small pieces, the size of whitebait.
Roll the fish in fine breadcrumbs till well covered, place it in a frying basket, plunge this in boiling fat, fry the fish for a minute or
two, taking care not to overcook it, drain on paper, arrange on a
fresh paper or d'oyley on a hot dish, dust with pepper and salt, and
serve at once.
Brown bread-and-butter and cut lemon should accompany this
dish, which should be garnished with sprigs of parsley.

SOURCE: AUSTRALIAN TOWN & COUNTRY JOURNAL,
1903

Mock Whitefish

½ pint milk
2 oz rice flour
Butter
Breadcrumbs
Parsley
Onion
3 potatoes
Egg

Bring to boil ½ pint milk and thicken with ground rice, to make a
little stiffer than for rice mould (I've no idea how stiff that is meant
to be, as I've never made a rice mould, but it stiffens up by itself to
a reasonable thickness).
Add a lump of butter, salt, a little grated onion and cook all together for 10 minutes, stirring frequently. Boil 3 potatoes and put
through masher, and while hot add to rice, or it will not set well.
Pour into a dish to stiffen, and when quite cold, cut into slices,
roll in egg and breadcrumbs, fry and serve with parsley sauce as a
fish course.

Note: The mixture must be thick, as the frying softens the rice.

SOURCE: MRS.E. W. KIRK, 1929

7
MOCK SAUCES & DRESSINGS

Mock Chutney

Mix Worcestershire sauce with apricot jam. Add a few raisins, soaked in a little warm water.

SOURCE: RATION BOOK RECIPES - 'MAKING DO'
BATHURST REGIONAL COUNCIL, NSW

Mock Hollandaise Sauce

2 tablespoons butter
1/8 teaspoon pepper
2 tablespoons flour
Few grains cayenne
½ cup milk
Yolks 2 eggs
½ teaspoon salt
½cup butter
1 tablespoon lemon juice

Melt butter, add flour and stir until well blended; then add milk, salt, pepper and cayenne, and bring
to the boiling point. Stir in the egg yolks, butter bit by bit, and lemon juice.

SOURCE: FARMER 1921

Mock Indian Chutney

Stone and mince very finely a quarter of a pound of raisins, chop three ounces each of onions and garlic, and put the whole into a mortar, together with a quarter of a pound of salt, two ounces of mustard seed, and eight drachms of good cayenne pepper.
Pound all thoroughly well until reduced to a paste. Pour a pint of malt vinegar into a saucepan, add a quarter of a pound of sugar, and a pound of sour cooking apples, peeled, cored, and sliced.
Boil until the apples are tender. Mix in very gradually with the pounded mixture, and when thoroughly amalgamated bottle and cork down tightly.

SOURCE: THE DAILY NEWS, PERTH, WA 1909

About Drachms
A drachm is a unit of weight formerly used by apothecaries, equivalent to one eighth of an ounce.

Mock Mayonnaise Dressing I

6 tablespoons flour.
1 cup boiling water.
1 teaspoon salt, or more.
¼ cup acid.
½ teaspoon mustard.
2 yolks of eggs.
Pepper.
1 cup oil (chilled).
4 tablespoons oil

Make a sauce of the flour, seasonings and 4 tablespoons of oil and water. Boil gently 3 minutes and pour into the well mixed eggs. Stir occasionally as dressing cools to prevent a crust from forming. When COLD, add acid, mix well; add the cupful of oil 1/3 at a time and after each addition beat hard with a Dover egg beater. This makes a very thick mixture, and can be used for garnishing as it does not soften so readily as a Mayonnaise dressing.

SOURCE: BLACKMAN, 1917

Mock Mayonnaise Dressing II

One small potato
One teaspoon of made-up mustard
Vinegar according to your taste
125 ml light olive oil
Salt and pepper

Peel and cook the potato. Mash it until very smooth and silky. Add mustard and a few teaspoons of vinegar to suit your taste While beating, slowly olive oil, then season with salt and pepper.

SOURCE: ANON

8
MOCK DESSERTS, PIES, CAKES

Mock Angel Cake

1 cup sugar
1/3 teaspoon salt
1 1/3 cups flour
2/3 cup scalded milk
3 teaspoons baking powder
1 teaspoon vanilla
Whites 2 eggs

Mix and sift first four ingredients four times. Pour on gradually the scalded milk. Fold in whites of eggs beaten until stiff, and add vanilla.

Turn into an unbuttered angel cake pan and bake in a moderate oven forty-five minutes. This is better for being kept twenty-four hours.

SOURCE: FARMER 1921

Mock Apple Pie 1

2 cups sugar
2 teaspoons cream of tartar
1-¾ cups water
Zest and 2 tablespoons juice from 1 lemon
1 package (14.1 oz.) ready-to-use refrigerated pie pastry (2 crusts)
36 Ritz Crackers, coarsely broken (about 1-¾ cups)
2 tablespoons butter or margarine, cut into small pieces
½ teaspoons ground cinnamon

Mix sugar and cream of tartar in medium saucepan. Gradually stir in water. Bring to boil on high heat; simmer on low heat 5 min. or until mixture is reduced to 1-½ cups. Stir in zest and juice; cool 30 min.

Heat oven to 425°F. Roll out 1 crust on lightly floured surface to 11-inch circle; place in 9-inch pie plate. Place cracker crumbs in crust. Pour sugar syrup over crumbs; top with butter and cinnamon.

Roll out remaining crust to 10-inch circle; place over pie. Seal and flute edge. Cut several slits in top crust to permit steam to escape.

Bake 30 to 35 min. or until golden brown. Cool.

SOURCE: KRAFT RECIPES

Mock Apple Pie II

2 cups water
2 teaspoons cream of tartar
25 crackers (preferably Ritz)
Uncooked pie shell

Bring water to the boil, drop in crackers. When they are soft, pour them into the pie shell and sprinkle with cinnamon.
Dab the top of the pie with small knobs of butter and bake in a moderate oven 180 C (350 degrees F) for about half an hour.

SOURCE ANON

Mock Apple Pie III

2 x Unbaked pie crusts
4 cups Water
1 ½ cups Sugar
4 teaspoons Cream of tartar
40 x Ritz Crackers
2 tablespoons Butter
1 teaspoon Cinnamon
¼ teaspoon Nutmeg
2 tablespoons juice and grated rind of 1 lemon

Boil water, sugar and cream of tartar. Add whole crackers, one at a time. Boil 2 minutes. Add remaining ingredients. Cool.
Pour into prepared pie shell. Cover with top pie-crust. Slit top for steam vents. Bake at 425 degrees F for 10 minutes. Reduce heat to 350 degrees. Continue to bake 20 to 25 minutes or until golden brown. Remove from oven. Cool.

SOURCE: ANON

Mock Apple Pie - Zucchini

Pie:
1 deep-dish unbaked pie-shell
4 cups zucchini; peeled, seeded and sliced 1/8" thick
¾ cup sugar
2 tablespoons tapioca
5 tablespoons lemon juice
½ teaspoon salt
2 teaspoons cinnamon
1 teaspoons nutmeg
2 tablespoons cornflour
½ cup sultanas

Topping:
½ cup butter, softened
½ cup sugar
½ cup flour

Mix all pie ingredients together and place in pie-shell. Combine the topping ingredients and pour on top of pie. Bake at 375 degrees F for one hour. Dot top of pie with butter.

SOURCE: FAMILY FAVORITES: AN ANNIVERSARY COOKBOOK (DATE UNKNOWN)

Mock Apricot Filling (for tarts)

Mix together grated carrot, plum jam and almond flavouring.

SOURCE: RATION BOOK RECIPES - MAKING DO
BATHURST REGIONAL COUNCIL, NSW

Mock Baked Egg Custard (when eggs are scarce)

Boil sago or rice in milk, or water and milk, thicken with custard
powder and sprinkle with grated nutmeg.
Bake until brown on top.

SOURCE: RATION BOOK RECIPES - MAKING DO
BATHURST REGIONAL COUNCIL, NSW

Mock Cabinet Pudding

Grease a quart basin and place round the inside some large raisins
stoned and split; three parts fill it with small pieces of bread, buttered or not, as wished.

Beat up an egg until light: pour over it three quarters of a pint of
new milk; stir in a pinch of salt and sugar to taste; pour this over
the bread; cover up and let stand an hour.
Tie a cloth over the basin and steam, or boil the pudding slowly for
an hour. Turn out and serve with any sweet sauce.

SOURCE: KYABRAM UNION 1889

Mock Cherry Pie

Mix one cup cranberries cut in halves, one-half cup raisins seeded and cut in pieces, three-fourths cup sugar, and one tablespoon
flour.
Dot over with one teaspoon butter.
Bake between crusts.

SOURCE: FARMER 1918.

Mock Fig Pudding I

Put 3 tablespoons of sago in a breakfast cup, and fill with milk, and
let soak about one hour.
Then add 1 cup of sugar, 1½ cups breadcrumbs, 1 tablespoon
melted butter, 1 cup dates, and, lastly, 1 teaspoon of carbon-
ate soda dissolved in a little milk. Mix thoroughly, and pour in a
greased mould, and steam 2 hours.
Serve with custard or cream.

SOURCE: THE QUEENSLANDER 1928

Mock Fig Pudding II

Take 4 tablespoons sago, 1 cup breadcrumbs, ½ cup milk, 1 tablespoon butter, ½ cup water, 1 cup dates, 1 cup sugar, ½ teaspoon
bicarbonate of soda.
Soak sago in milk and water for 1 hour.
Add sugar and breadcrumbs, melted butter, dates, and soda to sago
and water, mixing all well together.
Put in buttered mould and steam for two hours.   Serve with custard.

SOURCE: SUNDAY TIMES, PERTH, WA 1937

Mock Fig Pudding III

Soak 4 tablespoons of sago in 1 cup of milk overnight. Mix 1 cup
of breadcrumbs, 1 cup dates and 2 tablespoons sugar, 1 teaspoon
soda. Steam 2 hours. Serve with sauce.

SOURCE: BURRA RECORD, SA 1935

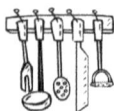

Mock Indian Pudding

½ small loaf baker's entire-wheat bread
3½ cups milk
½ cup molasses
Butter

Remove crusts from bread and cut into five slices of uniform thickness. Spread generously with butter, arrange in baking-dish, pour over three cups of milk and molasses. Bake from two to three hours in a very slow oven, stirring three times during the first hour of baking, then add remaining milk. Serve with cream or vanilla ice cream.

SOURCE: FARMER 1918

Mock Lemon Sponge

One and a half pints of cold water.
Two ounces of semolina.
Rind and juice of one lemon.
Sugar to taste.

Cook the semolina in the water for twelve minutes. Add grated lemon to taste. Pour into a large basin and beat till nearly cold. Turn into a wetted mould, leave till set, then turn out and serve with custard sauce.

SOURCE: THE ADVERTISER, ADELAIDE 1925

Mock Macaroons I

2 cups rolled oats
1 cup packed brown sugar
½ cup vegetable oil
1 egg
½ teaspoon salt
½ teaspoon almond extract

Mix together the first three ingredients in a bowl. Cover and allow to stand at least five hours, or overnight.

Pre-heat oven to 175 degrees C (350 degrees F). Grease an oven tray.

Add to the oatmeal mixture the egg, salt and almond extract. Mix thoroughly.

Drop rounded teaspoonfuls of the mixture about 2 cm apart on the greased oven tray. Bake for 7 or 8 minutes or until the middle is golden and edges are brown. Remove from tray and cool on wire racks.

SOURCE: ANON

Mock Macaroons II

Day-old bread, with crusts trimmed off.
Sweetened condensed milk
Desiccated coconut

Cut each slice of bread into four strips. Using two forks to hold the bread fingers, coat them with sweetened condensed milk and roll them in coconut. Bake them at 375° until browned.

SOURCE: ANON

Mock Macaroons III

Beat until stiff 2 egg whites, beating in ¼ teaspoonful salt, ½ tea
spoonful baking powder.
Fold in 1 cupful powdered sugar or 2/3rd cupful granulated sugar,
½ teaspoonful vanilla extract, 1 cupful chopped dates (or other
dried fruit), ½ cupful chopped almonds (or other nuts).
Drop by teaspoonfuls on thoroughly greased pans. Bake in a slow
oven until thoroughly done, lightly browned, which will be about
30 minutes. Remove quickly from pans with thin spatula.
This amount makes three dozen 1 ½-inch to 2-inch cookies.

SOURCE: NORTHERN TIMES, CARNARVON, WA 1938

Mock Macaroons IV

Mock macaroons must be baked in a moderate oven, and only until
delicately browned to have them of the desired consistency.
These dainty cakes go well with afternoon tea, or may serve as an
accompaniment to dessert.
Beat the white of one egg until light (but not stiff) and add gradually, while beating constantly, one cupful of brown sugar.
Cut and mix in one cupful of pecan-nut kernels finely chopped
and sprinkled with one-fourth of a tea spoonful of salt.
Drop from tip of spoon, one inch apart on a buttered sheet and
bake.
This recipe makes two dozen little cakes.

SOURCE: THE DAILY NEWS, PERTH, WA 1911

Mock Plum Pudding

1 cup grated raw carrot
1 cup grated raw potato
½ cup melted butter
1 cup sugar
1 cup flour
1 tsp nutmeg
1 tsp cinnamon
1 tsp salt
1 tsp baking soda
2 cups raisins

Mix carrots potatoes melted butter and sugar. Dredge the raisins in a little of the flour. Sift flour and mix with the other dry ingredients.
Add to the vegetables. Add dredged raisins
Place in a steamed pudding basin and fasten on the lid. Steam for 2 ½ hours or less if small moulds are used.

SOURCE:
'LEARNING FOOD ECONOMY', THE OUTLOOK 1916

Mock Plum Pudding II

Soak some stale bread in water, when thoroughly soaked, squeeze well and put in a basin with half cup currants, half cup raisins, one cup sugar, one packet mixed spice, few drops essence almonds, 2 large tablespoonfuls dripping, two eggs and some lemon peel. Mix all well together, put in a pie dish and bake for one hour.

SOURCE: THE DAILY NEWS, PERTH, WA 1907

Mock Plum Pudding III

2 cups stale cake crumbs
¼ cup hot milk
1 egg, well beaten
½ cup sugar
¼ cup molasses
2 tablespoons lemon juice
¼ cup cooked prunes, chopped
¾ cup seedless raisins, chopped
1 cup shredded tasty cheese
½ teaspoon nutmeg
¼ teaspoon baking soda
½ teaspoon ground cloves
1 teaspoon cinnamon
½ teaspoon salt
¼ cup flour

Foamy Sauce:
2 egg whites
1 cup icing sugar
¼ cup hot milk
1 teaspoon vanilla

Pour hot milk over cake crumbs. Add egg, sugar, molasses and lemon juice. Add spices, flour, soda. and salt which have been sifted together.

Fold in prunes and raisins which have been dredged with one teaspoon flour and shredded cheese. Fill buttered individual baking dishes or patty tins two thirds full. Bake in a moderate oven 350 degrees F. for 45 minutes.

If you wish, garnish with dried candied fruits.

Serve hot with foamy sauce made as follows: Beat egg whites until stiff, add sugar gradually and continue beating. Stir in milk and vanilla. Will make four large or six small servings.

SOURCE:
NAMBOUR CHRONICLE & NORTH COAST ADVERTISER, QLD. 1941

Mock Sago Plum Pudding I

Now that sago is an unknown quantity to buy, here is a very good substitute for the popular sago plum pudding:

Two tablespoons sugar, 2 tablespoons butter or good dripping, 2 tablespoons dark red jam and also some raisins, 3 teaspoon bicarbonate of soda dissolved in a cup of milk, sufficient plain flour to make a nice consistency.

Cream butter and sugar, add jam, then milk with the soda, and also raisins. Lastly add flour little by little. Steam in a buttered basin for three to four hours.

SOURCE: THE AUSTRALIAN WOMEN'S WEEKLY 1923

Mock Sago Plum Pudding II

Three tablespoons fine breakfast cereal
½ cup sugar
1 tablespoon shortening
1 ½ good cups breadcrumbs (wholemeal bread preferred)
Shredded lemon peel
½ cup sultanas
Little spice or cinnamon or nutmeg
1 cup milk
1 teaspoon soda dissolved in a little water.

Soak the cereal in the milk, which has been warmed. Stir in the sugar, shortening, breadcrumbs, etc.
Lastly, add the soda dissolved in water.
Place in a greased mould and steam 3 hours. Serve hot or cold with custard.

SOURCE: WORKER, BRISBANE, QLD. 1945

Mock Strawberries and Cream

Strawberries: Take 8 bananas, 2 tablespoonfuls strawberry jam, a little cream, and 1 teaspoonful brandy. Pulp the bananas and whip in the jam, the cream, and the brandy. Serve with custard or with mock cream.

Mock Cream: Beat the whites of 2 eggs to a stiff froth, then beat 2 tablespoonfuls butter with three-quarters of a cup of icing sugar until it is like cream. Add the whites of the eggs and beat all well together.

SOURCE: SUNDAY TIMES, PERTH, W A. 1922
'Second prize is awarded to Ruth. Brown, Pingelly, for recipe.'

Mock Quince - Stewed

Synthetic Quince - An Accidental Discovery
I put too much water with my rhubarb and had a whole dishful of beautiful pink juice left over, about a quart. In this I cooked some apples, quartered, and stewed till soft, and just as an experiment added a saucerful of strawberries--also "left over.
The result, being served, looked and tasted exactly like quince, except that the apple was a little softer.

SOURCE: CHARLOTTE PERKIN GILMAN
KLEBER, 1915

COOKERY

CORNER

9

MOCK MINCE PIES

Mock Mince Pie I

Two-thirds of a cup of rolled crackers, one cup of sugar, one cup of molasses, one-half cup of vinegar, one and one-half cups of boiling water, one cup of chopped raisins, butter the size of an egg, salt, one teaspoonful of cinnamon, and one teaspoonful each of cloves and nutmeg. After this has come to a boil and cooled, stir in two eggs.

SOURCE: WILLEY, 1884

Mock Mince Pie II

Six soda crackers, one-half cup of butter, one cup of molasses, one cup of currants, three cups of warm water, one cup of vinegar, two cups of raisins. Cook all together and spice to taste.

SOURCE: WILLEY, 1884

Mock Mince Pie III

Four Boston crackers rolled fine; pour on a cup of boiling water, and add one cup of sugar, one cup of molasses, one-half cup of vinegar, two eggs, two teaspoonfuls of extract of lemon, one-half teaspoonful of cloves and one teaspoonful of cinnamon.
Boil until it thickens. This will make two pies.

SOURCE: WILLEY, 1884

Mock Mince Pie IV

4 common crackers, rolled
1 cup raisins, seeded and chopped
1 ½ cups sugar
1 cup molasses
½ cup butter
1/3 cup lemon juice or vinegar
2 eggs well beaten
Spices

Mix ingredients in order given, adding spices to taste. Bake between crusts. This quantity will make two pies.

SOURCE: FARMER 1918.
#
Mock Mince Pie - Australian

Mock Mince Pie is a favorite; it is not too rich, and is easily made.
For it you will need some of your nice home-made sweet tomato
pickle. Chop enough of this to make half a cupful, first draining it
well, then add a cupful of chopped apples, half a cupful of brown
sugar, three-quarters of a cupful of chopped seeded raisins, two
table-spoonfuls of melted butter, one table spoonful of chopped
candied peel, one quarter cupful boiling water, half a cupful of
grape or currant jelly, with salt and spices to taste.
Mix all well, then bake between flaky pastry crusts. Custard Souffle
will perhaps appeal.

SOURCE: ADVOCATE, BURNIE, TASMANIA 1930

Mock Mince Pie Filling I

3 pints chopped apples
1 teaspoon clove
3 pints chopped green tomatoes
¾ teaspoon allspice
4 cups brown sugar
¾ teaspoon mace
1 1/3 cups vinegar
¾ teaspoon pepper
3 cups raisins
2 teaspoons salt
3 teaspoons cinnamon
¾ cup butter

Mix apples with tomatoes and drain. Add remaining ingredients, except butter, bring gradually to the boiling point, and let simmer three hours, then add butter. Turn into glass jars as soon as made.

SOURCE: FARMER, 1921

Mock Mince Pie Filling II

1 cup cranberries, chopped
1 cup raisins
1 cup corn syrup
2 tablespoons flour mixed with ¼ cup cold water
2 tablespoons fat

Mix all. Bring to boiling point and place in double crust pastry or cook until thick and use as filling for tarts.

SOURCE: GOUDISS 1918

Mock Mince Pie with Rhubarb

One cupful of rhubarb
1 cupful of raisins
1 lemon (grated rind and juice)
1 cupful of sugar
1 egg (well beaten)
¼ cupful of cracker crumbs
½ teaspoonful of salt.

Chop rhubarb and raisins, add the other ingredients and mix thoroughly. Line a sandwich tin with pastry, put in mock-mince, and cover with pastry.

Bake in a quick oven till paste is nicely browned.

SOURCE: BARRIER MINER, BROKEN HILL, NSW 1926.

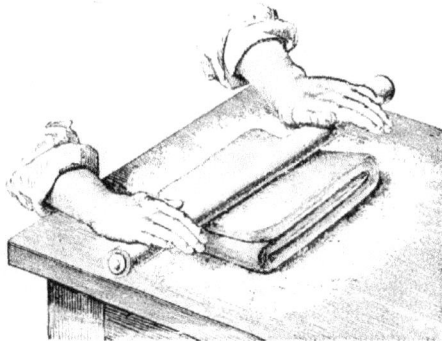

10
MOCK SWEETS & JAMS

Mock Almond Icing

Grate up half a pound of breadcrumbs to the finest possible size, add to this ¼ pound icing sugar, and one teaspoonful of almond flavouring, with the white of one egg to bind.

Mix it thoroughly and spread on the cake in the usual way.

SOURCE: THE BRISBANE COURIER, QUEENSLAND 1928

Mock Almond Paste I

4 oz soya flour
2 oz margarine or butter
5 oz castor sugar
5 oz icing sugar
½ cup water
Almond essence to taste

Simmer the soya flour in the water for 5 minutes or until all raw taste disappears.
Mix in the softened (not melted) butter or fat and rub in. Add the sugars and one or two dessertspoons of water till the mixture is a smooth paste. Add the essence.

Note: Mock almond paste can be used to fill chocolate Easter eggs.

SOURCE: THE SYDNEY MORNING HERALD 1947

Mock Almond Paste II
4oz Breadcrumbs
1 ½ lb icing sugar
Whites of 2 eggs
Yolk 1 egg
½ cup coconut
Almond essence
Lemon juice
A little sherry.

Sift icing sugar, work in bread-crumbs and coconut, mix to a paste dry dough with yolk, whites of eggs, lemon juice and essence, turn onto sugared board, and knead well. Roll out to required size, and cover cake under the icing layer.

SOURCE: THE AUSTRALIAN WOMEN'S WEEKLY 1939

Mock Almond Paste III

Four ounces very fine white bread-crumbs
8 oz icing sugar
1 teaspoon almond essence
White of 1 egg

Mix all dry ingredients, and make into a dry dough with the white of egg. Knead well. Use as required.

SOURCE: THE AUSTRALIAN WOMEN'S WEEKLY 1935

Mock Almond Paste with Coconut

ANXIOUS (Mitcham) wants to make mock almond paste using coconut.

For mock almond paste take 18 oz icing sugar, one heaped dessertspoon corn flour, 5 oz coconut one to two teaspoons ratafia essence, one good tablespoon almond oil, one dessert spoon lemon juice, 3 table spoons sherry or orange juice and the yolks of 2 large eggs.

Sift the icing sugar and cornflour, add the coconut, and mix lightly. Stir in the almond oil and essence, lemon juice, sherry (or orange juice) and the egg yolks beaten well together.

Mix to a fine consistency, but not crumbly, adding more sherry if required. Knead it on a pastry board sprinkled with icing sugar This quantity is sufficient for a half pound cake.

Almond oil can be obtained from a chemist.

SOURCE: THE ADVERTISER 1934

About Ratafia Essence:

Ratafia essence, used as a flavouring for food and drink, is usually extracted from almonds or the kernels of cherries, apricots, and peaches.

We have been unable to find a recipe for Ratafia Essence but here's one for Ratafia from Ellet's "Practical Housekeeper Containing 5000 Receipts & Maxims":

Ratafia.--Blanch two ounces of peach and apricot kernels, bruise and put them into a bottle, and fill nearly up with brandy.

Dissolve half a pound of white sugar-candy in a cup of cold water, and add to the brandy after it has stood a month on the kernels, and they are strained off; then filter through paper and bottle for use. The distilled leaves of peaches and nectarines, when the trees are cut in the spring, are an excellent substitute for ratafia in puddings.

Ratafia

This is a liquor prepared from different kinds of fruits, and is of different colours, according to the fruits made use of. These fruits should be gathered when in their greatest perfection, and the largest and most beautiful of them chosen for the purpose.

Red Ratafia

The following is the method of making red ratafia, fine and soft: Take of the black-heart cherries, 24 lbs., black cherries, 4 lbs., raspberries and strawberries. each, 3 lbs.; Pick the fruit from their stalks and bruise them, in which state let them continue 12 hours, then press out the juice, and to every pint of it add ¼ lb. of sugar.
When the sugar is dissolved, run the whole through the filtering-bag and add to it 3 quarts of proof spirit. Then take of cinnamon, 4 oz., mace, 4 oz, and cloves, 2 drachms. Bruise these spices, put them into an alembic with a gallon of proof spirit and 2 quarts of water, and draw off a gallon with a brisk fire.
Add as much of this spicy spirit to the ratafia as will render it agreeable; about ¼ is the usual proportion.

Dry or Sharp Ratafia

Take of cherries and gooseberries, each 30 lbs., mulberries, 7 lbs., raspberries, 10 lbs.; Pick all these fruits clean from their stalks, etc., bruise them and let them stand 12 hours, but do not suffer them to ferment. Press out the juice, and to every pint add 3 oz. of sugar.
When the sugar is dissolved, run it through the filtering-bag, and to every 5 pints of liquor add 4 pints of proof spirit, together with the same proportion of spirit drawn from spices.

Common Ratafia

Take of nutmegs, 8 oz, bitter almonds, 10 lbs., Lisbon sugar, 8 lbs, ambergris, 10 grs. Infuse these ingredients three days in 10 gallons of proof spirit and filter it through a flannel bag for use.

The nutmegs and bitter almonds must be bruised and the ambergris rubbed with the Lisbon sugar in a marble mortar, before they are infused in the spirit.

SOURCE: THE HOUSEHOLD CYCLOPEDIA OF GENERAL INFORMATION 1881

Mock Fondant Easter Eggs

Cook and mash and put through a strainer one medium potato.
Carefully measure ¼ cup mashed potatoes.
While potato is still warm add 1 tsp almond flavouring, 2 tablespoons margarine or butter. Sift together and add 1 cup powdered
sugar, ½ cup powdered milk, mix well and chill. After chilling
knead in enough powdered milk to handle well. Pack carefully into
empty egg shells using a salt spoon and packing down the mixture
till it fills the shell, smooth over the top.
Chill thoroughly for 24 hours.
Carefully peel off egg shell and decorate eggs using food colour-
ings, cinnamon or cocoa. Or dip in melted chocolate, chill and roll
in coloured sugar, or tie eggs with a pretty ribbon and add a small
icing sugar flower.

SOURCE: ANON

Mock Ginger I

Take 12 lb melon, six lemons, ½ lb green or 1 lb preserved ginger,
12 lb sugar, ½ lb. lime. Mix the lime with one gallon of water, and
when all that will not dissolve has settled strain off the clear liquid
through muslin.
Cut melon into 2-inch cubes, pour lime water over it, and allow to
stand for from six to 10 hours.
If the melon Is left too long in the lime water It will become hard,
so test frequently, and when the fruit is firm strain off the liquid.
Cut the lemons into slices, add them to the melon, also add the
ginger, sugar, and two and a half quarts of water.
Simmer very slowly, with lid on preserving pan, until syrup thickens. This may take as long as five hours. Bottle and seal.

SOURCE: THE ARGUS, MELBOURNE, 1936

Mock Ginger II

1 gallon Water
½ lb Lime
12 lbs Melon
2 quarts water
12 lbs Sugar
½ oz citric acid.

Pour 1 gallon water over ½ lb lime, let stand until clear, then strain through a piece of muslin or fine cloth, then pour over 12 lbs of melon cut into small cubes, and let stand over-night. Next day drain and put into preserving pan, and add 2 quarts of fresh water, 12 oz citric acid. Boil gently for 6 hours.

SOURCE: MIRROR, PERTH, WA 1923

Mock Ginger III

Recipe for crystallising melon with lime water.
Cut the melon into small strips and cover them with a liquid made of one dessertspoon of lime to a kerosene tin of water which has settled and been strained. Nest day make a syrup with enough water to cover the melon, allowing half a pound of sugar to each pound of melon. To flavor with ginger, allow 1 oz. of green or ½ oz. of dry ginger to the pound of fruit. Drain the melon and put into the boiling syrup. Cover and simmer till the melon is clear, then bottle, seeing that the syrup is over the top of the melon.

SOURCE: THE DAILY NEWS, PERTH, WA 1918

Mock Ginger IV - with Apple

Peel and cut in quarters six pounds of apples, six pounds of sugar, one-half pound of raw ginger. Pack the apples in a jar, a layer of apples, then sugar and ginger, and so on until all are put in.

Next day bruise one ounce of ginger and infuse it in a half-pint of boiling water, closely covered.

The day following put the apples, ginger, sugar, and the water from the bruised ginger, in a kettle and boil one hour, or until the apples look clear, and syrup rich.

Add some lemon peel cut very thin just before the apples are done.

SOURCE: HOWSON, 1881

Mock Ginger Jam

Three pounds vegetable marrow
3 pounds loaf sugar
1 oz ground ginger
Rind and juice of 2 lemons.

Peel marrow and remove seeds. Cut into pieces l inch thick and 3 inches long. Cut lemon rind very fine. Strain juice.

Put all in stewpan together, boil until clear - about 1 ½ hours.

SOURCE: THE AUSTRALIAN WOMEN'S WEEKLY 1940
'Consolation Prize of 2/6 to Miss L. Reddan,
Milton, 95 Trafalgar St., Stanmore, N.S.W.'

Mock Ice I

Dissolve half an ounce of Isinglass in a breakfast cup of hot water; beat up a pot of strawberry or any other preserve with a pint of cream, pass it through a sieve, add the juice of a lemon and a tea-cupful of sugar, then add the isinglass when nearly cold, whisk it together, and when it begins to thicken put it in a mould.

Mock Ice II

Dissolve one ounce of Isinglass in a little water, let it strain and cool. Put the juice of three lemons or half a pint of fruit jelly or fruit to one pint of cream, with some sugar - whisk, and add the cooled isinglass. Whisk again well, and pour into moulds.

SOURCE: WALSH 1859

Note: By 'ice' the Committee of Ladies means 'ice cream'.

About Isinglass
Isinglass is a substance obtained from the dried swim bladders of fish. These days agar-agar is used instead.

Mock Maple Syrup I

1 cup brown sugar
1 cup white sugar
1 cup water
3 tsp cornflour
½ tsp vanilla (or use maple extract instead)

Place sugars, water and cornflour in a pan and heat to boiling.
Remove from the heat and stir in vanilla or extract.

SOURCE: ANON

Mock Maple Syrup II

Take 1 cup light brown sugar, 1 cup water, pinch salt. Boil this for
1 minute, add 1 teaspoon vanilla essence. Serve hot or cold. This
is a nice change to serve with steamed puddings instead of jams
or sweet sauce.

SOURCE: SUNDAY TIMES, PERTH, 1934

Mock Maple Syrup with Honey

Mix 2 tablespoons of golden syrup with a tablespoon of honey,
a teaspoon of lemon juice and a tablespoon of boiling water. Stir
well and serve hot.

SOURCE: RATION BOOK RECIPES - 'MAKING DO'
BATHURST REGIONAL COUNCIL, NSW

Mock Marzipan I

2 oz of margarine
2 tablespoons of water
2-3 teaspoons of almond essence or flavouring
4 oz of sugar or golden syrup
4 oz of soya flour

Melt the margarine in the water, add the essence and sugar or syrup then the soya flour. Turn onto a board and knead well. Roll out; cut to a circular shape with the tin the cake was baked in. Smear the top of the cake with jam or jelly then cover with the marzipan.

SOURCE: ANON

Mock Marzipan II

2 tbsp white vegetable shortening (e.g. Copha)
1 tbsp light corn syrup
1 ½ lbs castor sugar, sifted
1 tsp almond extract

Place all ingredients into a large mixing bowl. Mix on slow speed of heavy-duty mixer until blended.
Shape into a ball and cover with plastic wrap.
Colour, shape and store just as you would for marzipan.

SOURCE: ANON

Mock Marzipan III

4 oz soya flour
4 oz sugar
2 oz margarine
2 small teaspoon almond essence
2 tbsp water

Melt margarine in a saucepan but do not burn. Add water, sugar and essence. Cook over low heat for 1 minute.
Stir in the soya flour. Turn out onto a board and knead well.
Useful for Christmas cakes

SOURCE: ANNE CHEALL
HTTP://WWW.FIGHTINGTHROUGH.CO.UK
#

Mock Marzipan with Semolina

1 cup semolina
1 cup castor sugar
1 teaspoon of almond essence
60 g butter, slightly softened
1 egg

Using your fingertips, rub the butter into the semolina until the mixture resembles fine crumbs.
Add the sugar and essence. Lightly beat the egg and add enough to the mixture to work it to a stiff paste.

*Note: Unlike real marzipan, Mock Marzipan can *not* be toasted or grilled.*

SOURCE: ANON

Mock Orange Marmalade 1

6 apples
Water
2 carrots, grated
2 tsp orange flavouring
Sugar

Chop the apples and put them in the jam pan. Barely cover them with water and bring to the boil. Leave simmering for 2 hours. Add a little extra water if it looks as if they will boil dry.

Strain the resulting pulp through a jelly bag and measure the liquid. Write down the amount.
Put the pulp into a pan and add in two grated carrots and two teaspoons of orange flavouring. Bring to the boil.

Measure out a quantity of sugar equal to the quantity of pulp and add it to the marmalade.

Bring back to the boil and check for the setting point. To test whether it has set, chill a saucer in to the fridge then drop a spoonful of marmalade on to the plate and put it back in the fridge for a few minutes. Push the edges of the marmalade with your finger - if it goes crinkly, then it has set.

When the marmalade has set, pour it into sterilised jars.

SOURCE: ANNE CHEALL
HTTP://WWW.FIGHTINGTHROUGH.CO.UK

Mock Orange Marmalade II

½ dozen firm carrots (3 cups)
1 ½ sour oranges
1 ½ pints sugar
Water

Wash and scrape the carrots and put through the mincer, cover with water, and boil one-half hour. Drain, and to each pint of carrots add one pint sugar and the juice and rind of sour oranges. Cook very slowly one hour, or until clear and thick.

SOURCE: THE QUEENSLANDER, 1931

Mock Raspberry Jam I

9 lb melon minced. Stand all night then strain off juice. Add 6 lbs sugar, boil till it jells. Add 1½ bottles raspberry cordial extract and 1 tin raspberry jam. Bring to boil. Bottle while hot.

SOURCE: RATION BOOK RECIPES - MAKING DO
BATHURST REGIONAL COUNCIL, NSW

Mock Raspberry Jam II

"Another Constant Reader" wants a recipe for mock raspberry jam. Peel and core 2 lb. quinces and put them through the mincer; pour boiling water over 3 lb. ripe tomatoes, and remove skins. Put tomatoes and quinces into pan with 5 lb. sugar and boil for 2½ to 3 hours; pot in usual way. This jam tastes like rich raspberry jam.

SOURCE: THE ADVERTISER, ADELAIDE 1937

Mock Raspberry Jam III

12 1b ripe tomatoes
9 lb sugar
1 bottle essence of raspberry
Cochineal.

Pour boiling water over tomatoes and peel them. Put into a preserving pan and add sugar. Boil until thick, then add raspberry essence. Remove from fire and colour to desired colour with cochineal. This is an excellent jam, and is equal to raspberry.

SOURCE: WESTERN MAIL, PERTH, WA 1945

Mock Raspberry Jam IV

Scald and peel 2 lb. of ripe tomatoes.
Peel, core, and grate of mince 3 lb. of quinces.
Put into preserving pan with 5 lb.' of sugar, and boil for two and a half or three hours, until a good colour.
This jam is similar to raspberry jam in flavour.
If the quinces are dry the peels and cores can be boiled and strained, and the juice (one or two cupfuls) added to the jam after it has boiled for one hour.

SOURCE: ALBANY ADVERTISER, WA 1936

Mock Strawberry Jam I

6 lb Tomatoes
one large pineapple
4 ½ lb sugar,
1 level teaspoon citric acid.

Scald and peel the tomatoes, cut them 1 inch large pieces, removing the hard part near the stalk. Cut the pineapple into small dice. Boil the fruit with one lb. of sugar for 20 minutes. Meanwhile heat the rest of the sugar in the oven. When it is very hot add it to the boiling jam. Boil all rapidly for three quarters of an hour or longer. A few minutes before taking up add the citric acid.

SOURCE: ALBANY ADVERTISER, W.A. 1936

Mock Strawberry Jam II

Strip and cut into slices a large bunch of rhubarb. Add a tin of preserved pineapple cut into small squares and 3 lb. of sugar. When nearly cooked add pineapple juice. Boil until a deep pink colour and remove when a little placed on a saucer will set.

SOURCE: THE QUEENSLANDER 1929

11
MOCK CREAMS

Mock Cream - Apricot

Beat together 1 tablespoon butter and 1 tablespoon sugar to a cream, add 1 tablespoon boiling water, 1 dessertspoon syrup from apricots.

SOURCE: BARRIER MINER, BROKEN HILL, 1935

Mock Cream - Banana

To make a delicious mock cream, slice a banana and beat with white of an egg until stiff and smooth.

SOURCE: THE AUSTRALIAN WOMEN'S WEEKLY, 1948

Mock Cream - Queensland

Warm half a-pint of new milk and when it is on the boil stir in a well-beaten egg. Turn out of basin to cool. You can hardly tell this from real cream. Any flavouring may be added to it, and a little castor sugar improves the taste.

SOURCE: THE BRISBANE COURIER, 1922

Mock Cream - Lemon

To make mock cream filling for cakes, take a cup of milk, a dessertspoon butter, essence of lemon, a tablespoon cornflour, a tablespoon sugar; moisten cornflour with a little of the milk.
Put remainder of milk on to boil. Stir in moistened cornflour and cook 5 minutes. Allow it to cool.
Beat butter and sugar to cream, add essence. Gradually stir in the thickened milk. Beat well.

SOURCE: ADVOCATE, TASMANIA 1929

Mock Cream - Plain

2 oz butter or margarine at room temperature
2 oz castor sugar
1 tablespoon dried milk powder
1 tablespoon milk

Beat the sugar and fat together until the butter turns white and looks creamy. Add the dried milk powder and milk and continue to beat well until the mixture is light and fluffy.

SOURCE: ANON

Mock Cream - Vanilla I

1 tablespoonful butter
1 tablespoonful sugar
1 cupful milk
1 tablespoonful cornflour
Essence to taste.

Beat butter and sugar to a cream, boil milk and thicken with corn-flour, then stand to cool.
When quite cold, mix in with sugar and butter; add essence to taste, ready for use.

SOURCE: SUNDAY TIMES, PERTH, WA 1923

Mock Cream - Vanilla II

A delicious mock cream -- Blend 1 dessertspoon cornflour with & little cold milk. Pour 1 cup boiling milk over and stir well. Boil for a couple of minutes. Cool. Cream 1 cup sugar and 1 tablespoon butter. Stir into cornflour mixture, add 1 teaspoon vanilla, beat well until it creams.

SOURCE: THE CENTRAL QUEENSLAND HERALD 1933

Mock Cream - Vanilla III

Soften ½ lb margarine in basin with 1 tablespoon boiling milk. Add ½ cup castor sugar and beat to cream for 5 minutes. Dissolve ½ teaspoon gelatine in cup with 2 tablespoons boiling water. Gradually add to creamed mixture until light and fluffy. Flavour with vanilla.

SOURCE: RATION BOOK RECIPES - 'MAKING DO' BATHURST REGIONAL COUNCIL, NSW

Mock Cream Vanilla IV

2 cups of milk
2 dessertspoonsful of gelatine
essence of vanilla
2 eggs,
2 dessertspoonsful of sugar.

Beat yolks of eggs and sugar together, place milk and gelatine in a saucepan, adding yolks of eggs and sugar. Place on fire and stir till nearly boiling, add essence, remove, and allow to cool. Then add beaten whites of eggs, mixing all thoroughly together.

An excellent cream for making trifle.

SOURCE: BARRIER MINER, BROKEN HILL, NSW 1935

Mock Cream - Vanilla V

1 ½ oz margarine
2 oz sugar
1 ½ level dessertspoons cornflour
¼ pt milk
Vanilla flavouring

Beat the fat and sugar to a soft cream. Mix cornflour to a smooth paste with some of the milk, heat up the rest and stir in the cornflour, bring to boil and cook slowly for 5 minutes, stirring continuously. Let it get nearly cold, stirring occasionally.
Beat this into the creamed fat and sugar gradually, beating well between each addition to keep it smooth. Flavour with vanilla to taste.

SOURCE: ANNE CHEALL'S WARTIME RECIPES
HTTP://WWW.FIGHTINGTHROUGH.CO.UK

Mock Cream Vanilla VI

125 grams margarine or butter
4 tablespoons of castor sugar
A little water
1 teaspoon of vanilla extract

Mix fat and sugar together well and whip for 5 minutes until white and fluffy. Add a teaspoon of vanilla essence and a little water if necessary to obtain creamy consistency.
Can be used as a scone topping or cake filler.

SOURCE: ANON

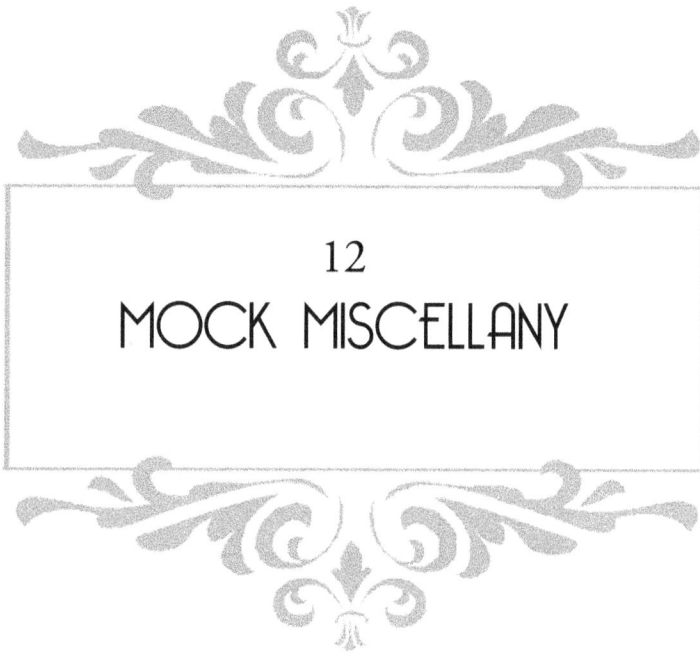

12
MOCK MISCELLANY

Mock Almonds (A soup garnish)

Cut stale bread in one-eighth inch slices, shape with a round cutter one and one-half inches in diameter, then shape in almond-shaped pieces. Brush over with melted butter, put in a pan, and bake until delicately browned.

SOURCE: FARMER, 1918.

Mock Bananas

Parsnips
Banana essence or extract
Sugar to taste

Choose young parsnips if possible for they are more tender and have a sweeter taste. Peel the parsnips, do not slice. Either cook in a small amount of unsalted water until tender or put into a steamer, cover and cook over boiling water.
If boiling the parsnips, then dry well on kitchen paper. If steaming the parsnips, simply remove from the steamer and dry.
Slice the cooked parsnips and put into a bowl and mash, add a few drops only of banana essence or extract. The easiest way to obtain a small amount of essence or extract is to dip a skewer into the bottle and then hold this over the bowl so the drops fall.
Continue adding banana flavouring until you get the right taste. Add sugar to taste then mash until smooth.
Use as a sandwich filling or as a pudding with yoghurt or custard.

SOURCE: ANON

Mock Cassava Bread

Remove crusts from a small, stale baker's loaf in four pieces, using a sharp, long-bladed knife; then cut in very thin slices lengthwise and shape with an elliptical cutter.

Dip each piece separately quickly in and out of cold water and shape over a form (using one-half-pound baking powder tins) and keep in place with soft twine. Place in dripping pan, brush over with melted butter and bake in a slow oven until crisp and delicately browned, turning frequently. Serve as an accompaniment to soup or five o'clock tea.

SOURCE: FARMER 1921

Mock Potatoes

4 oz haricot beans
1 parsnip
1 tablespoon flour
bacon bones
butter or good dripping

Soak the beans for 12 hours in cold water.
Drain and cook in boiling salted water until tender. A bacon bone greatly improves the flavour.
When the beans are cooked rub through a sieve and add 1 tablespoon flour and grated parsnip.
Season to taste and place in a well-greased pie-dish. Brush with butter or fat and bake in a moderate oven until golden brown.

SOURCE: THE CENTRAL QUEENSLAND HERALD 1943

Mock Souffle

New Australians living among us are introducing many novel recipes with cottage and cream cheese. Here is a golden 'crumb Fon-
due' looking like a mock souffle but tasting like a savoury custard
with a crumb texture.

Melt two level tablespoons butter in a small saucepan. Stir in two
level tablespoons plain flour. Add four tablespoons cold milk.

Stir just until smooth and thickening. At once add a small dessertspoon of grated raw white onion, 2 to 3 oz. of 'Ricotta' type
cottage cheese creamed with a fork, a scanty half sup of softly
crumbled stale white bread and a little salt and pepper.

Beat in two egg yolks.

Fold in the stiffly whisked egg whites. Bake in a shallow well-
greased pie-dish about 45 minutes in a pan of hot water in moderate (350 degrees F) oven.

Delicious with French beans. Makes three four servings.

SOURCE: THE ADVERTISER, ADELAIDE, SA 1952

Mock Yorkshire Puddings

Thick slices of stale bread put around the roast beef for the last 15
minutes or so makes an excellent substitute for Yorkshire Pudding.
Remove most of the fat before adding the bread and turn a couple
of times to brown nicely.

SOURCE: RATION BOOK RECIPES - MAKING DO
BATHURST REGIONAL COUNCIL, NSW

INDEX

MOCK CREAM 119

MOCK MISCELLANY 125

BIBLIOGRAPHY

Books

Bathurst: Ration Book Recipes - Making Do. Pub. Bathurst Regional Council, NSW, date unknown.

Baxter, 1913: Housekeeper's Encyclopedia. By Lucia Millet Baxter, Boston and New York, Houghton Mifflin company, 1913

Beeton, 1861: Mrs Beeton's Book of Household Management. By Isabella Beeton. Published Originally By S. O. Beeton in 24 Monthly Parts, 1859-1861. First Published in a Bound Edition 1861

Blackman, 1917: War-time Cookery - Practical Recipes Designed to Aid in the Conservation Movement. By Mrs Edith Blackman. Ypsilanti Press, Ypsilanti, Michigan USA 1917

Farmer, 1918: The Boston Cooking-School Cook Book. By Fannie Merritt Farmer (1857–1915) Rev. ed., with additional chapters on the cold pack method of canning, on the drying of fruits and vegetables, and on food values. Boston: Little, Brown, and Company, 1918

Farmer, 1921: A New Book of Cookery, by Fannie Merritt Farmer (1857–1915). Boston: Little, Brown, and Company, 1921

Corson, 1877: The Cooking Manual Of Practical Directions For Economical Every-day Cookery. By Juliet Corson, New York, Dodd, Mead & Co 1877

Goudiss, 1918: Foods That Will Win The War And How To Cook Them. C. Houston Goudiss and Alberta M. Goudiss, 1918

Harlan, 1875: Breakfast, Luncheon and Tea. By Marion Harland [Mary Virginia Terhune] 1875

Kirk, 1929: Tried Favourites Cookery Book With Household Hints and Other Useful Information. By Mrs.E. W. Kirk. Twelfth and Enlarged Edition. Edinburgh: J. B. Fairgrieve, 7 & 9 Cockburn Street, London: Horace Marshall & Son, 125 Fleet Street and Temple House, Temple Avenue, E.C. By Appointment to H.M. the King. 1929

Kleber, 1915: The Suffrage Cookbook. Compiled by L. O. Kleber. Fireship Press, 1915

Luck, 1915: The Belgian Cook-Book. Ed. Mrs. Brian Luck, E. P. Dutton, 1915

McKenzie Hill, 1909: Salads, Sandwiches and Chafing-Dish Dainties, With Fifty Illustrations of Original Dishes. By Janet McKenzie Hill, Editor of "The Boston Cooking-School Magazine" and Author of "Practical Cooking and Serving" NEW EDITION WITH ADDITIONAL RECIPES, Boston, Little, Brown, and Company 1909

McKenzie Hill, 1918: Economical War-time Cook Book: Wheatless Breads, Victory Breads and Rolls, How to Use Wheat Substitutes, How to Conserve Sugar, How to Save Fats, Salads, Canning, Etc., Etc. By Janet McKenzie Hill (1852-1933) George Sully & Company, New York 1918

Patten, 1985: We'll Eat Again: How the housewives on the Kitchen Front kept a hungry nation fed on nothing but rations. By Margaret Patten. Hamlyn; 1st edition 1985

Patten, 2004: Post-war Kitchen: Nostalgic Food and Facts from 1945-1954 by Margaret Patten. Hamlyn; New edition 2004

Walsh, 1859: The English Cookery Book, Uniting Good Style with Economy. Collected by A Committee of Ladies. ed. JH Walsh 1859

Willey, 1884: The Model Cookbook, Containing Over 1000 Thoroughly Tested Recipes. By Mrs Frances Willey, RH Lisk 1884

Newspapers

The Advertiser (Adelaide, South Australia: 1889 - 1931)

Advocate (Burnie, Tasmania: 1890 - 1954)

Albany Advertiser (Western Australia: 1897 - 1950)

The Argus (Melbourne, Victoria: 1848 - 1956)

Australian Town and Country Journal (NSW : 1870 - 1907)

The Australian Women's Weekly (1933 - 1982)

Barrier Miner (Broken Hill, New South Wales: 1888 - 1954)

The Brisbane Courier (Queensland: 1864 - 1933)

Burra Record (South Australia: 1878 - 1954)

Cairns Post (Queensland: 1909 - 1954)

The Charleville Times (Brisbane, Queensland: 1896 - 1954)

The Central Queensland Herald (Rockhampton, Queensland: 1930 - 1956)

The Daily News (Perth, Western Australia: 1882 - 1950)

Examiner (Launceston, Tasmania: 1900 - 1954)

Sunday Times (Perth, Western Australia: 1902 - 1954)

The Sydney Morning Herald (New South Wales: 1842 - 1954)

Kyabram Union (Victoria: 1886 - 1894)

Mirror (Perth, Western Australia: 1921 - 1956)

Morning Bulletin (Rockhampton, Queensland, Australia: 1878 - 1954)

Northern Times (Carnarvon, Western Australia: 1905 - 1952)

The Queenslander (Brisbane, Queensland: 1866 - 1939)

Townsville Daily Bulletin (Queensland: 1885 - 1954)

Western Mail (Perth, Western Australia: 1885 - 1954)

Worker (Brisbane, Queensland: 1890 - 1955)

Other Sources

Anne Cheall, http://www.fightingthrough.co.uk

The Ministry of Food (UK), 1939-1945

'Learning Food Economy' The Outlook, December 13, 1916

WEIGHTS & MEASURES

Conversion of Household Measures

Liquids

1 drop	¹⁄₂0 ml
1 teaspoon	5 ml
1 tablespoon	15 ml
1 cup	250 ml

Weights

2.20 pounds (avoirdupois)	1 kilogram (kg)
1 pound (avoirdupois)	453.6 grams (approx.500)
1 ounce (1/16 pound)	28.4 grams

Fluid Equivalents

1 fluid ounce (oz.)	29.57 ml (approx. 30)
1 pint (pt.) (16 fl. oz.)	473.2 ml (approx. 500)
1 pint, in the Imperial system	20 fluid ounces
1 quart (qt.)	946.4 ml (approx. 1000)
1 quart, in the Imperial system	40 fluid ounces
1 gallon (gal.)	3785.6 ml (approx. 4000)
1 gallon, in the Imperial system	160 fluid ounces

Metric System Weights and Measures

1 kilogram (kg)	1000 grams
1 milligram (mg)	0.001 gram
1 litre (l)	1000 ml
1 millilitre (ml)	0.001 l

Visit our Website
www.leavesofgoldpress.com

Spotted Dick

and Other Authentic Dishes
with Curious Names

Farrah Knight

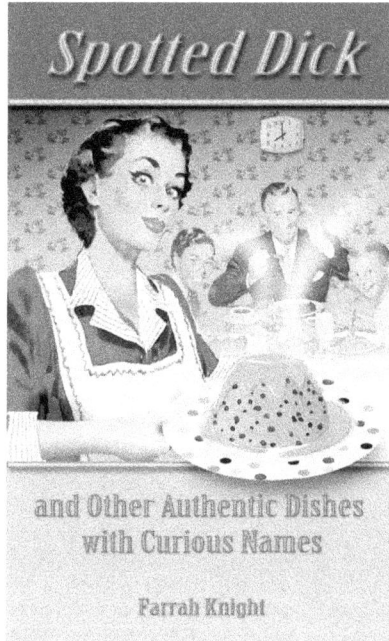

Have you seen the companion to this book?

SPOTTED DICK

AND

OTHER AUTHENTIC DISHES WITH CURIOUS NAMES

Including delicacies such as
.Devils on Horseback, Bedfordshire Clangers, Gooseberry Fool,
Apricots in Ambush, Dorset Knobs, Black Bottom Pudding,
Pigs in Blankets, Grasshopper Pie, English Monkey,
Impossible Pie, Bones of the Dead and Snickerdoodles.

Get the matching pair at all good bookshops

END

Cookery Notes

www.ingramcontent.com/pod-product-compliance
Lightning Source LLC
Chambersburg PA
CBHW021333090426
42742CB00008B/584